AF228358

Château

REAWAKENING

Tim Holding

Château

REAWAKENING

One couple's wild and wonderful journey
to save a crumbling French masterpiece

Hardie Grant

BOOKS

FOREWORD

I first discovered Purnon a long time ago. At that time it was a mysterious and inaccessible house, which had only been open to members of the aristocratic family who owned Purnon since 1893. I was aware of my privilege in being able to enter this place during that era; I was courteously welcomed to Purnon because I was the architect in charge of restoring another château that belonged to the same family in Burgundy. But the privilege extended further, to visit Purnon was to have the privilege of witnessing the last embers of a bygone world.

Desperate songs are the most beautiful songs: this verse by Alfred de Musset seemed to symbolise this place, a reflection of a refined way of life now gone, where past splendours gave way to present realities: leaking roofs, crumbling walls, abandoned outbuildings, deserted rooms with faded wall hangings ... and yet despite it all, the charm continued to shine. Everything at Purnon is a perfect harmony between landscape, architecture and decor.

When Tim and Felicity asked me to accompany them on the Purnon rebirth adventure, after they acquired it in 2020, their enthusiasm met mine: a dream was about to come true! But beware, waking up a two-hundred-year-old lady who has been dozing for so long requires not only energy - they both have plenty of it - but also tact and gentleness, which is needed to re-weave the invisible threads of history and authentically revive the flame of the 'genius of the place'.

Forty years in the service of France's heritage - working across the humblest Romanesque-chapel in Burgundy, to the most prestigious Palace of Versailles - have taught me many things about restoring heritage buildings: that you have to listen, know how to take the pulse of a building, to be attentive down to the smallest detail - this all 'makes' heritage. And in addition, at Purnon we have the inestimable good fortune that the archives were preserved, allowing us to decipher the memory of the place.

It was a miracle that the young couple agreed to *vivre sa maison* (live in their house) throughout the restoration process. This has meant camping a little every day and not giving in to despair on the dismal winter evenings when the wind and the rain infiltrates their home, as they run from room to room emptying buckets. However, they also have the good fortune of witnessing the spring light on the bright *tuffeau* stone, and of

undertaking explorations in the attic, the discoveries from which we then decipher together. An instruction followed to the letter: do not throw away any of these prosaic relics: old clysters, bed canopies or the scattered pieces of a billiard table. In short, we are looking to gradually understand the magic and intelligence of what others have created for us by putting the best of themselves into it: owner, architect, craftsmen and artists.

We follow them each in our role, with the awareness of a collective human adventure that forces us to surpass ourselves in turn, echoing those whose heritage we collect and perpetuate. Because even from the other side of the globe, as Tim and Felicity are, we are heirs of this place for as long as our hands are stretched out and our eyes attentive.

At the end of the eighteenth century, just as Purnon was being built for Monsieur and Madame Achard de la Haye, the France of the Ancien Régime was on the eve of the great upheaval of the Revolution. At the same time, Australia was being settled by Europeans. This beautiful and pure neoclassical château marks a culmination of these two worlds: Purnon was constructed just as the first buildings in the same style were being constructed in Sydney. Today it is new blood brought in from Melbourne in the form of Tim and Felicity to resurrect this corner of Poitou ... hence the phoenix rising from the ashes!

Today, the façades and roofs of the château are regaining their beauty - and their watertightness - and the park its splendour. The rooms are becoming welcoming, complete with bathrooms, and all with absolute respect for heritage and the history of this building. In short, life takes back its rights. We are all proud and thrilled to share this great adventure, and thank all the protagonists who contribute to it: Tim and Felicity first and foremost; the Ministry of Culture and the Fondation du Patrimoine who actively support the project; all the businesses and craftsmen of excellence who spare no effort; and finally all those who, on *les journées du patrimoine* (heritage open days) and on many other occasions, come to demonstrate their attachment to this exceptional place. There is still a long way to go to accomplish everything, but it is all the easier when it is done together.

Frédéric Didier, *architecte en chef des monuments historiques*, 2023.

Monsieur Frédéric Didier - *architecte en chef des monuments historiques* - studies some of Purnon's extraordinary eighteenth-century wallpapers.

CONTENTS

Introduction

AIMER, CE N'EST PAS SE REGARDER L'UN L'AUTRE, C'EST REGARDER ENSEMBLE DANS LA MÊME DIRECTION.

Love is not to gaze into each other's eyes but to gaze together in the same direction.
Antoine de Saint-Exupéry

This is the story of our journey to save Château de Purnon. But at its heart it's also a love story, because such a journey only has meaning when shared with someone who gazes in the same direction, however crazy and improbable that direction may be. And so although the words that follow are my own, Felicity and I have walked every step of this journey together. And, like any adventure, through its sharing it has been immeasurably enriched.

When we started, we dreamed of a place that we could share with family and friends - dining that captured the spirit of a bygone age, walks in the park on a warm, sunny day, or perhaps evenings relaxing with a glass of wine in one of the château's grand rooms.

But, just as in life, the journey has a way of becoming the destination.

When we left Australia more than a decade ago, we sought a life working and studying abroad. After an exhilarating but gruelling twenty-year career in politics, I wanted the chance to have a different life while I was still young enough to make a change. For Felicity, with a well-established online business, it was a chance to see whether the life of a digital nomad was really possible. Both of us wanted to see more of the world and learn more about ourselves.

We worked, studied and travelled: an aid project in Vanuatu, a master's in international relations in Paris, language courses across four continents. We had our highs and lows. And then one day our journey brought us here, to a tiny hamlet in a part of France few tourists ever visit. To a beautiful but crumbling château and a community that has welcomed us warmly.

Saving Purnon has asked more of us than we could possibly have imagined. The work has often been physically demanding and the progress painstakingly slow. We have acquired new skills taught patiently to us by the remarkable artisans who have accompanied us on this quest. And, perhaps surprisingly, we have learned to leverage skills from the careers that we left behind in coming to France.

Uncovering Château de Purnon's beauty is exciting. But equally rewarding has been uncovering her story. The people who lived and worked here have faced revolution, war, and economic and social turmoil over two and a half tumultuous centuries. Much of this history has been passed to us directly. Fading memories mean that this is perhaps the last chance to capture these amazing stories.

We could not save Purnon alone - the volunteers and professionals who have worked with us can be proud of all that has been accomplished so far. Alongside our life savings we have been generously supported by the French government, philanthropic organisations and friends and supporters.

When we acquired Château de Purnon, she lay in peril. She still does. But with each step, we know that we are reawakening a gem of French architecture.

People ask why and expect a pithy answer. The account that follows is as succinct as I could manage.

We hope, as you follow our journey so far, that you too can gaze in the same direction as Felicity and me, and perhaps feel the same sense of fascination, pride and accomplishment. Château de Purnon is worth it.

Our journey to save Purnon has taught Flick and me as much about each other as it has about architecture or history.

Dedicated to my father, Bruce, who,
as an accountant, would have begged us not to
purchase a crumbling château and, as a father,
would have shared every step of our journey
with unwavering passion and enthusiasm.

THE PATH TO *Purnon*

IL NE FAUT PAS S'EMBARQUER SANS BISCUIT.

You must not set off without rations.
(Don't engage in an enterprise lightly.)

There are more than forty thousand châteaux in France, the vast majority in private hands. Today, thousands of these extraordinary buildings are in peril.

The huge edifices make utterly impractical homes. Hundreds of years old, impossible to heat and badly wired, they occupy vast estates that are difficult to maintain. Coupled with French inheritance laws that divide ownership between expanding numbers of family members with each generation, this means that French châteaux are in crisis.

With each passing decade, deterioration accelerates and the costs of preservation and restoration climb, so the rising interest in purchasing and preserving these buildings amongst a band of intrepid custodians is to be welcomed.

What sort of person buys such a place?

You probably love France and are fascinated by France's rich history. You must have a sense of adventure and an enormous appetite for work. It helps to have family and friends who indulge your optimism and encourage you to chase your dreams.

Above all, you must be a little crazy. Buying and restoring a crumbling French château makes absolutely no financial sense. It will break you physically and fiscally. French bureaucracy is not for the faint-hearted. Whatever timelines and budgets you set, everything takes longer and costs more. Some dreams will not be realised in your lifetime.

But you will be part of an endeavour that will leave a legacy long after you are gone. When we walk around Purnon today, we admire the trees planted by people who would never live to see their full splendour. We give thanks that people of vision had the generosity to build something for those who would come after them. Could they ever have imagined that some of those people would be from a place thousands of kilometres away, from a country undreamed of by them?

We called it château porn. Alone and often at night, I would search the internet with mounting excitement. Grand French châteaux, with marvellous descriptions and amazing photos, at implausible prices. Twenty-four bedrooms, eighteen bathrooms, Louis the something or other slept here, sixty-five hectares, large lake … I would lose myself in the fantasy of what it would be like to actually own one of these magnificent buildings.

I have never considered myself a dreamer, but I do confess to a slightly obsessive personality, and unrealistic plans can sometimes take hold. Much to Flick's annoyance, I would interrupt whatever she was doing with a currency converter in hand to read out the amazing descriptions of properties that I had unearthed. While outwardly acknowledging the absurdity of it all (if only to affirm that I had not lost all grip on reality), inwardly, a plan started to form. Could we really own one of these extraordinary properties for around the price of our tiny Paris apartment? How much would it cost to restore? How would we decorate literally dozens of rooms? Maintain the grounds? Could we tackle a project for which we had no experience and few practical skills?

Purnon's fragile stonework - just one of a myriad of restoration challenges.

BUYING AND RESTORING
A CRUMBLING FRENCH
CHÂTEAU MAKES ABSOLUTELY
NO FINANCIAL SENSE.
IT WILL BREAK YOU PHYSICALLY
AND FISCALLY.

Purnon's southern façade has been battered by time,
but her sublime harmony and elegance endure.

Like a love-struck teenager, I would develop crushes on particular châteaux. When I would return to searching after an absence of a few months, the relief at finding a favourite still on the market was palpable.

It was during a visit to Corsica and over a superb dinner nestled in the mountains that Flick finally called my bluff. I had been waxing lyrical about one particular object of my passion, offering ideas about the business possibilities that owning such a château might create, when she suggested we call the agent and arrange an inspection. Imagine my shock upon discovering the following day that this château, with whom I had conducted a wholly unrequited long-distance love affair over the last five years, had been sold the previous week!

But we were now bitten by the château bug. And we realised that if this was to be the path for us, something a little more systematic would be required.

We both love French architecture. We find French history fascinating and the culture captivating. But were we really ready to commit to a project restoring and then maintaining a piece of French history?

So we started with an open conversation about the appeal in owning and restoring a château. For both of us, certain architectural styles were more attractive than others. We definitely preferred the harmony and symmetry of neoclassicism when compared to the more practical defensive fortified castles of earlier eras. And, yes, we wanted a certain 'wow' factor – hard to define, but you know it the instant you see it. If we were going to commit years of our life and our sweat and savings, we needed to absolutely adore the property we were working on.

Flick loves horses, so working stables or ones that could be restored held out the prospect of pursuing one of her life's passions. For me, principal rooms with large volumes and high ceilings would provide a wonderful backdrop for pursuing a growing interest in French interior decorating. Both of us secretly hoped that we would find a château with a private chapel that we could use to host a wedding with friends and family.

As we started searching, we came to realise that we wanted a certain amount of land around the château to afford a level of privacy and control over our project. But we also knew that owning vast tracts of agricultural land or forest may present management issues that were beyond us.

To the surprise of many, we were not fixated on any particular region in France. Since neither of us are Russian kleptocrats or Saudi oil princes, we would have to work within a budget for the purchase and restoration of our château that roughly equalled the money that we could obtain from the sale of the Paris apartment and of a small townhouse in our home town of Melbourne. And we discussed the risks – the financial risks as well as our own lack of restoration expertise.

With these parameters in mind, we began our search. We started online, systematically compiling lists of properties that met the criteria above. It's not easy, as none of them are identified by their château name but rather by unhelpful town locators that are often dozens of kilometres away. This is done not only to protect the privacy of the sellers but also to safeguard the considerable commissions that flow to the agents who market these properties. Understandably, they don't want potential buyers approaching their clients directly.

After finding several dozen matching our criteria, we wrote to agents seeking dossiers that provided maps, cadastral plans and more detailed information and photos about the properties. With this information in hand, Google Earth searches often revealed problematic neighbourhood issues, like major expressways that punctuated key panoramas or neighbouring agricultural uses that might significantly impact on local amenity.

As we refined our list, we started to group the promising ones together geographically and organise inspections.

Looking through a château is enormous fun but also time-consuming. It takes at least a full day to conduct a worthwhile inspection that can be the basis for making an offer. This is a huge commitment for owners, agents and prospective buyers alike, and we didn't want to gain a reputation for wasting people's time.

We started in Normandy, on the north coast of France. The first was a nineteenth-century château owned by some Eastern European plutocrat. The château itself was amazing, located inside a walled park offering unparalleled privacy. A chapel, beautiful stables and huge principal rooms saw our excitement grow. But there was something amiss. Much of the wood panelling in its principal rooms had been removed. Holes had been punched in many floors and walls – we were told it was to ascertain their condition! Tapestries and carpets crafted specifically for several of the rooms had been removed, apparently in order to protect them. It was difficult to clarify where they were now and whether it would ever be possible to reunite them with the château. And then we spotted the unmistakable signs of *champignons*, a wood-consuming fungus whose growth can cause catastrophic and irreparable damage. But to our then untrained eye, this did not seem like an insurmountable problem.

Purnon's Lebanese cedars – a towering testament to the vision of the generation that established our beautiful park.

And, yes, we wanted a certain 'wow' factor – hard to define, but you know it the instant you see it.

Purnon's breathtaking natural setting offers a stunning view over the Forêt de Scévolles.

We chatted with the agent about the price - it was clearly very negotiable. But we were shocked by the scale of the project we would be taking on. Years later we laugh, both at the size of the venture we would ultimately embrace and the bullet we dodged by avoiding those *champignons*!

Next was another Normandy château, this one with the remnants of a Second World War German V-1 missile launching site on the property. From the attic we inspected the roof, amused at the strange pride the owner seemed to take in showcasing the partially restored wooden frame and slate tiles. We would quickly come to realise that assessing and comprehending the state of the roof was perhaps the single most important factor in ascertaining the true scale of the project that a prospective chatelain is taking on.

We travelled south to a small village near Bordeaux and an eighteenth-century château built on fourteenth-century foundations. This secluded property enjoyed incredible views over the river Garonne, and the *boiseries* (wood panelling) in the principal rooms were stunning. However, poor succession planning had led to the sell-off of neighbouring tracts of land that once protected the château's privacy. It would become a common tale.

Not surprisingly, the Loire Valley yielded some beautiful properties. Just north of Orléans we found a sublime château surrounded by a beautiful moat and gorgeously arranged gardens. Again, poor decisions about the sale of a neighbouring farm would mean sharing a section of the property very close to the château with the large wall of a farmhouse that looked like a junkyard. We were not willing to cede control over our project to such dishevelled neighbours.

Afterwards we overnighted at Château de Freschines. Once the home of Antoine Lavoisier, considered the father of modern chemistry, it was in the early stages of a comprehensive restoration being undertaken by a friendly Austrian family. It seemed appropriate that our somewhat insane search for a French château should find us hunkered down for a night in a former asylum. The warm welcome of the new owners only slightly offset the ominous melancholy that seemed to hang over the property.

A trip west to Brittany offered two fascinating prospects. We always enjoyed visits that included the château's actual owners. You learn so much more about a property when people who live there show you through. As we knocked on the door of the first, a rather dignified but decidedly friendly chap appeared. He spoke impeccable English but with a vaguely exotic accent. Within minutes he confessed that he was a descendent of Russian aristocrats who had fled the country in the aftermath of the toppling of the tsar.

Unusually, no interior photos had been available online. As he led us through the rabbit warren of rooms, it became apparent that this was to protect the existence of a remarkable private art collection gracing every available space on the walls of this amazing property. It included not only nineteenth-century portraits of his ancestors but also several modern art pieces of some note.

Every room was packed with objets d'art. An incredible silver samovar balanced precariously on a Louis XIV desk with boulle inlay. Beautiful wallpapers and fabrics from renowned interior designers decorated tiny alcoves and stairways. From atop a steep hill, the château overlooked a picturesque canal.

Vodka was produced and, before we knew it, we were being regaled with some version of the life story of our entertaining host. He had been married, he claimed, to a princess of Liechtenstein. It hadn't worked out. He apologised for the state of his art collection - some of the better pieces were on loan to the Hermitage in St Petersburg. I tried to empathise. I suppose it could happen to any of us.

But as the vodka warmed our throats and the sales pitch finished, the shortcomings were obvious. Internally, the building was shambolic. The rooms were impossibly arranged, evidenced by a completely impractical kitchen that had been added in one of the château towers. Centrally located kitchens are a modern contrivance. In great homes, the kitchens were the preserve of domestic staff and cooks, so there was no need to place them at the heart of family life as we would today. Instead, they were typically found in basements. Finding a suitable place for a good-sized kitchen is often one of the most perplexing challenges facing the contemporary chatelain. Our Russian host had failed dismally.

Both of his large *dépendances* (outbuildings) had also been sold off. These buildings, only a few metres from the château, were now home to complete strangers. It seemed bizarre to us to own hectares of terrain and yet share your driveway and courtyard with people with whom you had no connection.

The next day saw us visiting a château for which I had high hopes. It had the wonderful harmony that reflected the architectural style we were seeking. An amazing interior stone staircase - by far the most impressive we had seen - created an entrance of true splendour. It boasted its own hall of mirrors and rooms with great proportions that testified to a thoughtful and tasteful restoration. Meticulously planned French gardens graced the back of the château. It had stables and a chapel. I felt like we were onto a winner. Flick was not so sure. We returned for a second visit a few weeks later and completed a short hike from a nearby village that took in great views of the château. We chatted with the owners.

Virgin and Child - silent witnesses to the gradual decline of Purnon's chapel.

As we shared lunch afterwards in the village, Flick finally struck upon what was missing. 'There's no project,' she observed. 'What will we do? Surely our ambition goes beyond restoring a couple of promising barns. We would simply be buying someone else's completed project.' She was right. We were not just purchasing a home – we were embarking on an adventure to save and restore something in peril. This was not the château for us.

Just out of Alençon, we came upon a small but beautiful château. Rather unusually, it was actually two châteaux of equal proportions arranged across a courtyard. Bounded by the river Sarthe and with the most impressive *pigeonnier* (dovecote) we would ever see, we were in love again.

It was small and manageable with many projects to occupy us. It had a chapel, a lake and wonderful views. We would be a few minutes' drive from the village of Saint-Céneri-le-Gérei, one of the designated 'most beautiful villages of France' (yes, there's an official list).

After a second visit, we made an offer. We were bidding against a British school looking for a small French campus who were awaiting planning approvals from local authorities before their negotiations could be finalised. In the end, we could not agree on a price that would have left us with the resources to restore and then furnish the château. We would have to walk away. Even today we follow the adventures of the owners online after the sale to the school did not proceed.

We were starting to lose hope. Perhaps our expectations and budget did not align (do they ever in real estate?). We had conducted so much research that when helpful agents tried to suggest new properties to show us, we already knew of them and why we had ruled them out.

Our visits had taught us what to look for. First and foremost, the state of the roof. Not only the tiles themselves (typically slate) but also the *charpente*, the giant oak frame that supports the immense slate cover. Restoring roofs is easily the single most expensive project in any major château restoration. We learned to ignore the general state of the interior but check for evidence of significant water or fire damage.

We noted the age and condition of electricals. Rewiring huge châteaux is expensive and vital if insurance cover is to be affordable. Be aware of the age of the *fosse septique* (septic tank system). Older systems will need to be replaced when larger works are being carried out to comply with modern regulations. Note the heating system. Even if you plan to change it, you may have to live with the existing system for several winters. Try to

identify significant land subsidence issues. Look for major cracks in stonework that may be evidence the building is still moving.

Was the property heritage-listed? And if so, exactly which elements? Heritage listing may confirm the architectural and historical significance of the château but brings the burden of complying with heritage rules. The grants and tax breaks you will be eligible for may be negated by the regulatory approvals required when altering paint colours or seeking to double-glaze windows. What sort of activities were your neighbours engaged in? We found one beautiful château that had to contend with the odours of a neighbouring pig farm. How close is the nearest *boulangerie*? A very important consideration if you wish to enjoy a freshly baked baguette or warm croissants each morning.

Most importantly, we had to try to imagine how practical daily life would be in our home. Châteaux were designed as grand statements of social prestige. They were built in an era when wealthy people employed many servants to cook, wash and even dress them. These hard-working souls cooked and served, cut and carried firewood in the winter and washed clothes and sheets by hand in outdoor laundries. We had to picture modern life in our château – where would we cook, eat, sleep and wash? How easily could we live our lives across potentially thousands of square metres of château living space?

There was one last property on our list, an eighteenth-century château not far from the town of Châteaubriant in Brittany. This château was separated from its large forested estate by a public road. Our hearts sank as the inspection progressed and we realised that, for various reasons, this was not to be our château.

We came across a bathroom on the ground level where an enormous hole was being excavated through the floor. Apparently the current owner had calculated that his cellar's odd layout was evidence of a secret chamber that must lie underneath this bathroom. He was determined to dig his way through – the proof of his so far fruitless quest lay chaotically before us. Further into our tour we came upon the owner himself, a lonely figure huddled in one of the few rooms of the château that he was trying unsuccessfully to heat. Unappetising cans of food were stacked on the shelves. It was a sad and sobering reminder of the realities of château life for many people who can't find a buyer for an estate that is utterly beyond their financial and physical resources.

Our search appeared to have reached a dead-end. We had visited fifteen unique and wonderful properties, and our visits had helped us to better understand exactly what we were seeking. But we were becoming disheartened.

One of Purnon's many mysteries. Who is the subject
of this portrait? We are yet to find out.

And then, there she was.
Like a thunderbolt, or coup de foudre.

We were in a subdued mood as we started the long drive back to Paris with Guillaume, our enthusiastic real estate agent. He quizzed us again about our requirements and started to describe a possibility. I was sceptical. We had reviewed everything online. If it really fitted our criteria, why hadn't I seen it? 'It's complicated,' Guillaume replied. 'It's not online because there has been disagreement amongst some of the family members about the sale. And it's got a lot of problems. Serious problems.' As Flick drove, he flicked through his phone to open the dossier.

And then, there she was. Like a thunderbolt, or *coup de foudre*, as the French would say.

I would love to claim that the first time we laid eyes on Château de Purnon she was bathed in perfect blue sky or that mist rose slowly over the *grand allée*. But in truth, it was on a phone screen in a hire car, while our real estate agent listed the various problems that explained why she had never been listed online.

And we knew, we just knew, that despite the problems and Guillaume's reservations and scepticism, we had to go and see her.

Château de Purnon. Despite all of her problems she has stolen our hearts.

NO *Turning* BACK

QUAND LE VIN EST TIRÉ,
IL FAUT LE BOIRE.

When the wine is poured, one must drink it.
(Once the first step is taken, there is no going back.)

19 MAY
'Voilà! La clé du paradis ... j'espère!'

La Comtesse Nicole de Rochequairie grandiloquently hands over a huge key 'to paradise' worthy of a château. Her hesitating 'I hope' will prove not entirely misplaced as the journey ahead will take Flick and me both to paradise and to places more akin to Dante's inferno.

The search for our dream château had taken us to sixteen extraordinary domains. But it was Château de Purnon on the edge of the Forêt de Scévolles in Haut Poitou that stole our hearts.

Built just before the French Revolution and set on a little over twenty hectares, Purnon gazes north across the forest. Perfectly aligned with the château lies the *grand allée*, a three-kilometre corridor that pierces the woods. It is a stupendous private view that is only discernible from the château. The *grand allée* is longer than the Grand Canal at Versailles, as our heritage architect Monsieur Didier likes to remind us. And he should know - he is, after all, the *architecte en chef* at Versailles.

Purnon's neoclassical design emphasises symmetry and harmony, with the château arranged around a *cour d'honneur* (main courtyard) flanked by two grand outbuildings. It's a breathtaking setting that lifts your heart after even the most strenuous day of château toil.

On the western side, one outbuilding is home to an extraordinary chapel split over two levels. It also houses stables with several tack rooms. On the eastern side sits a building with more practical uses: garages for our tractors, an old *boulangerie* (it is France, after all), accommodation for farm workers and even an old *buanderie* (laundry).

The château itself is spread over three principal levels as well as cellars and an attic. It is flanked on three sides by a dry moat and arranged with two wings joined by a central axis, like a squat letter H.

Today the château is changing hands for only the second time in its history, and to foreigners, no less - *quelle horreur*! But the de Rochequairie family, whose great-grandfather purchased Purnon in 1893, has welcomed us warmly. Eleven descendants inherited Purnon upon the passing of the Marquis Gilles de Rochequairie in 2013. One of his sons, Pierre, chokes back a tear as we arrive, testifying to the private anguish that must rack noble families forced to make heartbreaking decisions and let such properties leave the fold.

As the sun rises over Purnon on our first day as the château's new owners, our removalist van arrives and begins disgorging the contents of our tiny Paris apartment. By the time we packed up, the apartment was heaving with our purchases from le Marché aux Puces and the Drouot auction house. We plan to live in one small wing of the château's ground floor where, we are assured, the heating and lighting still work. The family has thoughtfully cleared a couple of rooms for us. Our furniture is dwarfed by the huge volumes of the rooms.

We have agreed with the de Rochequairies' request for a further two months to clear their final possessions from Purnon. An antique dealer named Serge and his team are already on site, stripping some of the more valuable items that were not part of the château's acquisition.

We've negotiated to purchase some of the château's machinery and tools for maintaining the grounds and parks. We will shortly discuss the purchase of a range of furniture items and paintings that we are eager to keep at the château.

But first, a makeshift buffet appears – baguette, jambon and a bottle of wine. Pierre, a keen hunter, produces a homemade *sanglier* (wild boar) terrine. We open a bottle of Australian red and its contents are carefully appraised by intrigued French palates. They approve.

We now proceed to the negotiations over furniture items. An absurd procession commences through the house.

Most of the truly valuable items were sold several years ago. But it's difficult to appreciate just how much remains crowded across thousands of square metres of the château's various levels.

It's a tricky game. Most of the items are, frankly, not worth much. I'm keen to safeguard sentimental things that speak to the lives of the people who have lived here – portraits and busts and so on. Flick is drawn to fabrics, some of them handwoven. If original, they should provide a hint to how rooms, windows and beds were originally decorated. But in truth, we're amateurs. We don't really know what is original or what particular pieces are truly worth.

To complicate things further, the various items have been divided amongst different branches of the family. Marked by sticky labels, they at least give us a clue – the unlabelled items have no specific claimant and are probably not regarded as valuable. They will perhaps be left behind for us.

But with French and English being freely exchanged, the negotiations quickly descend into a farcical Tower of Babel. 'How much is this?' I ask, pointing to an old commode. Someone consults an inventory. '*Deux cent euros.*' Two hundred euros – it's a ridiculous price. '*Faire une offre,*' (make an offer) someone else chimes in. Puzzled, I repeat what I think I've heard. 'Fair enough?' It sounds almost the same as the French phrase. Confusion reigns.

Our patient real estate agent, Guillaume, is a graduate of the École du Louvre. He is an expert in eighteenth-century French interior design. He is also, to our surprise, unflinchingly honest. His expertise helps us identify the hundreds of items on the family's list scattered randomly throughout the building. Despite standing to receive a modest commission on the sale of any furnishings, he quickly dismisses many of the valuations proffered on the list.

Serge and his team hover hungrily, apparently poised to strip the château of its last vestiges of original furnishings should we fail to agree. Having spent a lifetime engaged in the coercive negotiation tactics of politics, I have to secretly admire the efficacy and menace of this particular bargaining technique.

In the end we are able to agree on a respectable list. It includes an epic Napoleon III *tapis* (carpet) that graces the *grand salon*, the vast dining room table, various family portraits and even, incongruously, a plaster bust of Louis XVIII, one of France's least celebrated kings.

The negotiations stumble on a few matters – we cannot agree on a price for the château's enormous archives. We believe we have secured the actual plans of the château, but the personal papers of the Achard de la Haye family who built the château and those of the de Rochequairie family are another matter. Those discussions are postponed for another day.

The curtains in the *grand salon* also prove problematic – one of the branches of the family claims to have already sold them to an antique dealer in Montpellier. Legal advice is sought, and according to French law they don't form part of the fixtures. We had secured many pieces during our original purchase negotiations but, sadly, the *grand salon* curtains will be lost to the château forever.

Previous page: Our new home glimpsed through the 1812 gate.
Left: In many rooms time has stood still.

Eventually, the last of our guests disappear. For the first time, Flick and I can explore our new home alone.

In its heyday, Purnon would have required a significant population to support the château and the surrounding farming lands and hunting forest.

As well as the château and the two large *communs* (outbuildings), we've acquired an old *chai* (barrel room) in which grapes grown locally would have been pressed, barrelled and fermented.

A small farmhouse, several large barns, pigpens, chicken coops, a ruined *orangerie* and a swimming pool precinct complete the main compound. At the back of the château, an English park extends over several hectares.

About four hundred metres south of the château lies the Moulin Bigeard, a seventeenth-century mill complete with a ruined *pigeonnier* (dovecote). Adjacent to the *moulin* is a large semi-walled potager garden and orchard with a small *pavillon de potager*. It's a delightful building, decorated inside with agricultural motifs on its plasterwork. It would have housed tools and equipment to maintain the potager. An Éolienne Bollée (a late-nineteenth-century wind turbine) towers over the potager, evoking a vaguely science-fiction ambience. The wind turbine and adjacent pump house would have delivered water to our *château d'eau* (water tower) and in turn fed six large water basins in the potager.

The domain is surrounded by several kilometres of stone walls. We've bought everything inside the walls, as well as an access driveway at our rear gate and a portion of the *grand allée* that pierces the forest.

We purchased Purnon after only one day's exploration the previous November. It was, of course, impossible to even scratch the surface of such a large estate in such a short time. Over the coming months, fresh discoveries will be unearthed almost every day.

The tack rooms.

IN THE CHAI WE COME ACROSS AN ELEGANT NINETEENTH-CENTURY HORSE CARRIAGE.

Flick and I wander through the buildings a little dazed. We randomly open cupboards, in equal parts delighted and shocked. In the *chai* we come across an elegant nineteenth-century horse carriage, while the château storage yields carefully starched maids' uniforms and the marquis' detachable collars and cuffs, prams, bidets and baths, baking trays for madeleines … It's an Aladdin's cave bursting with two hundred and fifty years of treasures and mysteries.

The enormity of what we have taken on is starting to sink in. Finally, we slump exhausted into bed.

20 MAY

We awake to the sound of birdsong. It's a far cry from the hubbub of Paris, with its sirens and traffic. I prise open the casement window latches and shutters and gaze at the spectacle of four *chevreuils* (roe deer) grazing nonchalantly in our English park. It's a dreamy view. Is this really our new life? Messages arrive from the de Rochequairie family checking that we have survived our first night, a sweet gesture.

Excited, we don our work clothes and gaze out at the beauty of the *grand allée*. It seems impossible that we are now the owners and custodians of this incredible estate. A heavy burden of responsibility weighs on us. We are eager to set to work.

Pierre arrives with a document that explains how the water, electricity, plumbing, gas and heating systems work. We wander the property, identifying the various pipes, taps and meters. Nothing works quite as expected - everything has a little twist or trick that reflects two centuries of ad hoc repairs and renovations. We try to understand all the technicalities. It's a lot to take in, and the scope for misunderstanding in a foreign language is wide.

Pierre, a retired colonel in the French army, evinces a deep love for Purnon. We will later learn that he had investigated purchasing the Moulin Bigeard for his family many years ago. He opted instead to buy and restore La Gloriette, a beautiful nineteenth-century stone farmhouse only a few minutes away.

Pierre regales us with tales of life here when he was a boy. He remembers a bell chiming on the side of the château that summoned scattered children back for lunch. The brass bell is still there. He recalls the storms of 1999 that felled many enormous Lebanese cedars in the château's English park and the despair of his father as he surveyed the havoc wrought.

We will often wonder why the de Rochequairie family resolved to sell such an incredible gem. Part of the explanation lies in the intricacies of French inheritance law. When ownership of the property passed to an ever-expanding group of relatives, the responsibility for meeting the significant maintenance costs (insurance, utilities, park upkeep, taxes and so on) started to impact on branches of the family who spent little or no time here.

The Moulin Bigeard - a farmhouse more than a century older than the château itself.

The scale of the works required will be immense. The extraordinary roof of the château is only a few years away from total collapse. The stone façades are crumbling and weatherworn.

As Purnon deteriorated over the decades, the resources to restore her grew beyond the capacity of any one branch or the shared willingness of the family collectively. Eventually, the château had to be sold. It's a common story in contemporary France.

The scale of the works required will be immense. The extraordinary roof of the château is only a few years away from total collapse. The stone façades are crumbling and weatherworn. Several of the huge outbuildings are in a fragile and perilous state. Plumbing and electricals will require complete replacement. The vast park is suffering from decades of neglect.

Marshalling the resources to restore Purnon will be a mammoth task, far beyond the private resources of Flick and me. We will need to collaborate with the French government as well as find clever ways to fundraise and leverage philanthropic support. Ultimately, we will have to commit all of our savings. It's a daunting and somewhat reckless decision. Without months of expert study, it is impossible to know how much the restoration is going to cost. At some stage our money will run out. But we are determined to save Purnon for future generations.

A glimpse of Purnon from the *boulangerie*.

21 MAY

Today we receive a visit from Daniel Bouquet. For twenty years he has been employed by the family to protect the château and maintain the park. Working one day a week, it is a completely impossible task. He's retiring and has come to explain our two tractors and the various power tools that we've purchased with the château.

A career in politics has taught me many things, but operating farm equipment is not one of them. I try to conceal my complete ignorance of all things mechanical. The tutorial is further complicated by Monsieur Bouquet's unintelligible regional patois. He smiles continuously – he's either Haut Poitou's friendliest soul or he's completely bemused by the thought of me trying to operate this equipment.

Purnon's three garages are his domain. He knows exactly where everything is and what it is for. The more obvious items are clear to me – chainsaws, hedge trimmers, lawnmowers – but the various tractor attachments powered by the tractors' hydraulic systems are a complete mystery. Every imaginable fuel, oil and antifreeze is present. Different oils for the tractor, chainsaw, hydraulic system, even a specific oil for the air compressor. A covered automotive pit lies beneath the floor of the central garage. I find myself wondering whether I will ever have sufficient expertise to get underneath one of our tractors.

I dismiss the thought. It's ludicrous.

A clear take-out from the lesson is that I must change the various oils when required. 'How often?' I ask after each explanation. 'From time to time,' Monsieur Bouquet helpfully responds.

I tentatively approach the Renault 461. Built in 1972, the tractor is the same age as me. That is all we have in common. Despite its age, I'm assured it works magnificently. Strangely, the first and second gears don't function – from reverse, the gear shifts immediately to third to proceed forward. Monsieur Bouquet assures me that this should give us no trouble. I'm doubtful.

After a few hours, the lesson is finished. I gratefully proffer a bottle of Australian wine as thanks. Monsieur Bouquet is nonplussed. I fear that I have committed some severe social faux pas. He departs, no doubt anxious about the fate of his carefully maintained equipment.

In the *communs ouest* the craftsmanship of those who originally built Purnon can still be admired more than two centuries later.

I slump on the steering wheel, defeated. Why did we buy a château? What were we thinking?

I climb onto the Renault. It starts and I back her out of the garage. I'm terrified of damaging our precious stone terraces as I proceed tentatively towards Purnon's long southern driveway where I calculate I can do the least harm. So far so good. I change gears and increase the throttle to pick up speed, my confidence growing. Fool's courage!

I try to slow on the forest path. The gears are stuck! I'm lurching forward rapidly and start to troubleshoot. Which is the brake and which is the gear shift? Large trees beckon on either side.

I veer off the path, depressing every available pedal and cutting the engine at the same time. The screaming engine stops. I take stock – everything appears okay. I'll just back her out, return to the garage and try again another day. The Renault engine coughs back into life. The reverse gear isn't working! I'm stuck in the woods and can only go forward, but my path is blocked by trees. I slump on the steering wheel, defeated. Why did we buy a château? What were we thinking?

Then I have a brainwave. The chainsaw! I can cut my way out and exit using the remaining forward gear. I set to work felling several perfectly innocent trees, poor victims of my incompetent tractor skills.

I'm halfway through when I notice someone staring from a nearby gate. I switch the chainsaw off and wander over. It's our neighbouring farmer. He's curious about Purnon's new owners and has arrived to introduce himself. As we chat through the gate, he notices the Renault parked oddly in the middle of the woods. He seems pleased that the new owners have set to work so quickly to clear the mass of overgrown trees but puzzled at the random spot I've selected to commence this herculean task. I'm too ashamed to admit that the tractor is stuck. I'm sure he could fix it in minutes, but I can't bring myself to be introduced to him in this way.

He departs and I can get back to work. Soon I've freed the tractor and I return the Renault to the garage. I feel it's a small victory. For months afterwards, when I pass the felled trees in the woods, I feel pangs of guilt.

Purnon's ardoise (slate) roof and the massive wooden frame that supports it is a masterpiece of late eighteenth-century architecture. Its dilapidated condition will also be the source of unimaginable misery.

Above: The *chevilles* that secure the *charpente* in the Philibert de l'Orme style.
Right: The extraordinary roof frame of the *communs est*.

22 MAY

Purnon's *ardoise* (slate) roof and the massive wooden frame that supports it are masterpieces of late eighteenth-century architecture. Its dilapidated condition will also be the source of unimaginable misery for Flick and me.

The château roof has been constructed in the style of Philibert de l'Orme (1514-70), a celebrated French architect of the Renaissance era. He worked on many great French châteaux, such as Chenonceau, Fontainebleau and the Tuileries Palace. But during his time, France was facing a growing shortage of the immense oak trees that furnished the beams of the palaces and castles of this era.

One of his greatest innovations is evidenced in the roof at Purnon. He invented a system of construction that utilised small curved pieces of wood in the erection of roof frames. This reduced the cost and increased the speed at which châteaux could be constructed. He used *chevilles* (carefully crafted wooden pegs) to hold the frame together. His methods experienced a revival at the end of the eighteenth century and are showcased in our château. The roof at Purnon is amongst the finest examples of his method of construction in a private building in France today.

The two immense *communs* also house exceptional roofs in the Philibert de l'Orme style, this time in the shape of an inverted ship's hull. The frames are works of art of national significance.

Purnon's roof sits atop an attic organised into three sections. On the eastern and western sides we can admire the *charpente* directly (the internal wooden frame that supports the *ardoise* tiles). But in the centre is a vast room with a vaulted ceiling in plaster and a *tomette* floor. It is the château's largest room and its original use is a mystery to us.

The greatest risk in any château purchase is the state of the roof. We've bought Purnon knowing that restoring the roof is a project of the utmost urgency. But we can only guess at the expected cost. We can see the gaps in the tiles where light streams through. In some cases, leaks have already rotted the oak beams, and holes in the attic floor permit us to stare forlornly into the second storey below. Unchecked, rain will accelerate the château's decline.

Soon, 3D imaging, some of it captured with drones, will enable experts to truly comprehend the roof's condition. In the meantime, it leaks badly whenever it rains. An ad hoc system of buckets and old pots captures as much as possible. When heavy rains arrive, it will be a constant battle to manage and improve this system until our roof can be secured for the major works.

23 MAY

Alongside the Renault, Purnon's second tractor is an ancient International that I'm using to maintain our lawns. It's a capricious beast. The cutter works well but the massive cage that I need to connect behind it to catch the mown grass is of dubious value. Trying to attach and detach it is systematically crushing my fingers. Of course, Daniel Bouquet made it look easy.

The tractor's huge size and large turning circle makes it difficult to manoeuvre around Purnon's buildings and fragile stonework.

There is clearly something I don't understand about its power system. Each time I turn the engine off for more than a couple of minutes, it won't restart and I have to remove the battery and stagger back to the garage to recharge it. I never knew how heavy tractor batteries could be.

But when Purnon's lawns are freshly cut, I have to admit they look amazing.

The upper floors of the château with the condition of the slate roof clearly visible.

24 MAY

With a vast château extending over several floors and a couple of thousand square metres of living space, it's often disappointing for others to learn that our daily living is confined to a relatively compact space on the eastern part of the ground floor. We have a bedroom and bathroom with low ceilings because of the old staff quarters directly above these rooms. The low ceilings will make them easier to heat during the cold winter months. A large living room known as the *salon d'hiver* (winter living room) is served by a fireplace, one of several that we had cleaned as soon as we arrived. Purnon's original kitchens are huge and sit in the basement. They were still being used well into the 1960s. But we use a kitchenette dating from the 1970s. It's tiny, and as we try to prepare meals in its cramped space, we are constantly brainstorming how we can create a kitchen area that can serve as a hub for modern living.

Flick has a small office that rather usefully looks out onto the *cour d'honneur* so she can easily spot any visitors or deliveries.

Our one indulgence is that, due to the layout of the château, all of our meals are taken in Purnon's huge *salle à manger* (dining room). Sitting opposite one another, we are dwarfed by the massive table but become quickly accustomed to the comical spectacle of dining like royalty while dressed in our heavy-duty work gear. We resolve that wherever on the property we are working, we will always stop and return to the château for a sit-down lunch or dinner. We could all learn from the French custom of taking time for a cooked meal and a proper break at lunch. No self-respecting French person would be caught scoffing a sandwich in front of their computer screen. And at dinner, it's wonderful to sit around the magnificent dining room table and recap the day's events.

Centre: Purnon's *salon d'hiver* (winter salon) was originally the bedroom of the marquis and the marquise who constructed the château - a very modern living arrangement for that era.
Right: Grand dining in the *salle à manger*.

We become quickly accustomed to the comical spectacle of dining like royalty while dressed in our heavy-duty work gear.

25 MAY

After several days of exploring and planning, a strategy is starting to develop.

Despite our impatience, we can't be everywhere. We need to focus.

Within the château we have around two thousand square metres of space. We have thousands more spread across a dozen other buildings and more than twenty hectares of woods, prairies and gardens.

Inside the château, we must wait. Despite the dilapidated state of many of the interior rooms, with the leaking roof we risk carrying out work that may ultimately be wasted. Just minor works so that we can live here safely in the short term. We must reconcile ourselves to a somewhat frugal and at times uncomfortable existence. By waiting we will gain the benefit that comes from living in a space before deciding how best to use different rooms.

Fixing the roof will be the first and most urgent task and, along with the stone façades, the most expensive. But it's not a project we can tackle ourselves – we must wait for the professionals.

In the meantime, we can commence an inventory of more than two centuries of trash and treasure and begin the painstaking process of disposing of those things that really are rubbish. I'm soon on first-name terms with the gentlemen at the local *déchetterie* (tip).

We must reconcile ourselves
to a somewhat frugal and at times
uncomfortable existence.

Decay on the château's second floor.

WE START TO NOTICE LONG-FORGOTTEN PATHS AND EVEN BUILDINGS THAT HAVE BEEN SWALLOWED BY THE TREES.

Around the grounds, decades of neglect mean that we must get to work immediately. Some buildings are threatened by overhanging branches. For others it is too late, roofs have collapsed and trees are already emerging from within that will need to be felled.

At first glance, the grounds around the estate are beautiful to wander through. Completely overgrown, there is a real sense of discovery and adventure as we come across nineteenth-century farm machinery that has laid concealed in the woods for perhaps a hundred years. But the estate was never supposed to look like this. It was designed in keeping with the fashion of the time as a *parc anglais*.

Characterised by open spaces, rolling meadows and pockets of trees, the English park style conveyed a sense of randomness, but in reality it was planned precisely. This new fashion was a reaction against the formal and symmetrical parterres of the *jardin à la française* that had preceded it.

We try to see through the jungle that has emerged and the kilometres of wire fences that now crisscross the property. We can see the epic trees – oaks, Lebanese cedars, lime trees, chestnuts, some hundreds of years old – that give a hint as to how the property was supposed to look. We start to notice long-forgotten paths and even buildings that have been swallowed by the trees.

And amidst the chaos, we begin to turn our minds to how we might live here and reintroduce this amazing place to the world and share it with others.

The task to rediscover her will be immense.

In the *basse-cour* (farmyard) several buildings have already been lost to nature and neglect.

Monsieur Didier on a regular site visit.

30 MAY

We've appointed our heritage architect. This is the single most important decision we will make on our journey to save Purnon. He is Monsieur Frédéric Didier, *architecte en chef* at the Château de Versailles. He comes highly recommended.

On arrival, he bounds out of his car with obvious enthusiasm and begins a tour of Purnon that sees him exploring every nook and cranny of our incredible home. Indifferent to his personal safety, he ascends ramshackle staircases we had been too nervous to tackle. His experienced eye quickly identifies features that had escaped our untrained gaze. It is his infectious enthusiasm and astonishment at the quasi-original state of so much of Purnon that seals it for us. He is the person that we want to guide us on this amazing adventure. Our journey ahead will have many ups and downs, but our decision to appoint Monsieur Didier is one that we will never regret.

We are bursting to start, but Monsieur Didier urges patience.

'We are reawakening an old lady who has been asleep for a long time; we must wake her slowly,' he cautions.

Nevertheless, Monsieur Didier swings immediately into action. He contacts the de Rochequairie family directly and negotiates with them to prevent the further plundering of original furnishings by Serge and his team, who have returned several times. He arranges for the inspection and copying of the most important sections of Purnon's vast archives so that the vital secrets they harbour can inform his work on understanding the design and construction of the buildings. Perhaps he can also solve the mystery of the identity of the château's original architect.

Monsieur Didier's first instruction is that the *grenier* (attic) – packed literally to the rafters with more than two centuries of paraphernalia – will need to be painstakingly emptied. It's a necessary step to begin preparations for the restoration of Purnon's *ardoise* roof. It will also enable us to start identifying exactly what lies hidden in our massive *grenier*. It's a task I'm up for.

'We are reawakening an old lady who has been asleep for a long time; we must wake her slowly.'

EIGHTY-EIGHT STAIRS LIE BETWEEN THE GRENIER AND THE GROUND FLOOR.

Eighty-eight stairs lie between the *grenier* and the ground floor. I know this exactly because it's a trip I will make more than three hundred and fifty times over the next few weeks as we clear the three vast spaces in the *grenier*. Beds, *ciels de lit* (canopies), luggage, an old marble fireplace, *boiseries*, giant wardrobes stuffed with old bed linen and clothes ... a seemingly endless procession testifying to the lives of the aristocrats and their domestic staff who lived at Purnon during the eighteenth and nineteenth centuries.

Monsieur Didier leads us to one corner of the *grenier*. 'What do you think this is?' he asks, pointing to a series of very old hand-carved wooden supports.

I proffer a guess. 'It looks like some sort of workbench.'

'Look more carefully,' he urges. I notice odd scalloping in the corner. 'It's a billiard table,' he declares. 'A very old billiard table. Those are the pockets. I've never seen anything like it. It must be protected.'

He's right. And unbelievably, as the attic slowly clears, other pieces of the table begin to emerge. First the four cross pieces that caught Monsieur Didier's eye, providing the eight original table legs. Then we uncover the four pieces of the frame that give the table its exact dimensions. Remarkably, their felt lining secured by tacks has survived through the centuries. Then, suspended in the roof itself, we spot the system of wooden channels that would have guided the pocketed balls to a collection point beneath the table – traces of their felt lining provide the hint that they form part of the table. My excitement grows. Upon closer inspection, several rough poles in one remote corner reveal themselves to be handcrafted cue sticks. Suddenly I recall seeing others leaning casually against a wall with some curtain rails on the second floor. Before long, I've collected six of varying lengths. When Monsieur Didier returns for his regular visit, we reveal the reconstructed table to him. He is astonished. It's the last surviving example of its kind in France. Only a copy exists at the Petit Trianon at Versailles – the original was lost during the Revolution.

And then it's our turn to be surprised.

The central room in our *grenier* had puzzled us all. It has a huge vaulted plaster ceiling and at over sixty-six square metres is the largest room in the château. It traverses the house from north to south with glass windows at each end. Surprisingly, it houses a fireplace, an odd luxury in a space usually reserved for domestic staff.

Monsieur Didier informs us that he has been carefully studying the château archives and this room with its beautiful tomette floor was, in fact, the billiard room. We are determined to one day restore the table and return her to her original home – the huge room designed especially for her.

Centre: The fireplace in the attic billiard room, dwarfed by the vaulted plaster ceiling.
Right: Gradually the pieces are reunited. This wooden pocket was the clue that revealed the billiard table's original purpose.
Following page: The original eighteenth-century billiard table frame rebuilt from pieces scattered across Purnon's attic.

1 JUNE

Purnon sits on the cusp of the unfortunately named village of Verrue ('wart' in French).

The commune with the surrounding hamlets is home to around four hundred people. It's a tiny village, and an ancient one - records first mention Verruca more than a thousand years ago.

Today Pierre is introducing us to the newly elected mayor, the wonderfully energetic and enthusiastic Monsieur Francis Siclet. His mother, born in Verrue, is on the cusp of turning one hundred and is Verrue's oldest inhabitant. Monsieur Siclet keeps a pack of hunting hounds, and at feeding time we can occasionally hear their enthusiastic barking from the château grounds.

His connection with Purnon is strong. Surprisingly to us, in light of its terrible condition, Monsieur Siclet reveals that decades ago he used to live at the Moulin Bigeard inside the château grounds. He's thrilled that new owners will now commence the restoration of Purnon - locals have been anxious about the fate of the château for many years.

5 JUNE

We're craving some level of comfort and normalcy in our strange new lives. Boxes that arrived full of our stuff from Paris and Australia are still stacked in dusty corners of the château.

Opposite our bedroom is a huge room of wardrobes that once served as a dressing room. We set to work. First the old junk comes out, then the garish 1970s shelf linings are removed. After a deep clean, the cupboards can be treated against wood borers and then oiled. Shelves and railings are repaired and the plaster on the ceiling patched and painted. And then suddenly, after several days of work, we have more clothes-hanging space than either of us have enjoyed in a lifetime! We can start to unpack!

6 JUNE

Purnon was constructed at an elegant and refined time in French architecture. Grand dinners during the earlier eras of Louis XIV and Louis XV were huge spectacles of social prestige, and large entertaining rooms were required to accommodate the guests. By contrast, Louis XVI was a shy man and dining became more intimate and private. As a consequence, the size of principal rooms in grand châteaux came to reflect this more subtle mode of entertaining.

At Purnon, guests would have arrived on the château terrace with an epic view of the *grand allée* stretching out behind them. Alighting from their carriages, they would have been swept through the main entrance, into the *entrée* and then directed right into Purnon's antechamber. Perhaps they would have paused here while their social status and title were confirmed. Calling cards might have been exchanged; we found a small collection of eighteenth-century cards from Monsieur Achard de La Haye, the château's original owner, hidden in a box at the back of a cupboard.

Guests might then have been invited into the *grand salon*, a splendid light filled room that occupies the north-west corner of the château. At the time of the château's construction, the room would have been decorated in the Louis XVI style like the rest of Purnon. But at the end of the nineteenth century when the château was purchased by Daniel de Rochequairie, a rococo revival was underway and this room alone was altered. Curves and sculpted mouldings were added to the straight lines. A huge iron fire back was installed in a new fireplace with the coats of arms of the de Rochequairie and Le Lou families. It must have been brought to Purnon from another château, and dates from 1722 when these two noble families were joined in marriage.

Atop the *boiseries* sit six paintings. Two are pastoral scenes and one is a classic still life of grapes, perhaps pointing to Purnon's history of wine production. Opposite is another still life, this one depicting game, perhaps a nod to the château's hunting past.

A curtain tieback in Purnon's *grand salon*.

The other two paintings contain classical images alluding to science that puzzle us. After careful research, we discover that they are painted reproductions of panels that graced the Paris apartment of the Duc de Picquigny, an eighteenth-century French soldier and scientist. The originals were executed by Jacques de Lajoue, a celebrated French architectural painter. One, *L'Optique*, contains allusions to Archimedes' mirrors, which were used to defend the city of Syracuse during a Roman siege. This fascination with inventions from antiquity was common during the Age of Enlightenment. The other, *La Géographie*, features a huge globe studied by finely dressed scholars.

We love the *grand salon*, and discussing how we might bring life back to her with tasteful furnishings is great fun.

Perhaps some guests would have been invited into the next room, the château's *bibliothèque* or library. It is now home to a wonderful grand piano that we plan to restore. From Monsieur Didier's careful study of the original floor plans, we learn that this room has also changed. It was originally two rooms - one dedicated to *trictrac*, an eighteenth-century version of backgammon, and the other once part of a suite of rooms that formed the apartment of Monsieur Achard de la Haye's mother-in-law. Atop a hidden, narrow and steep staircase requiring a knotted rope to ascend, we discover the room of madame's *domestique* (servant). It's a tiny, dark and dusty alcove with a small bell for summoning her as required. It might be only a few steps from the *grand salon* but a vast gulf separated the social classes at Purnon.

The *grand salon* - modified at the end of the nineteenth century to reflect a rococo revival.

10 JUNE

Exiting by car from the château's village gate, we catch our neighbour José de Penaranda surreptitiously cutting the verges of this section of our driveway on his ride-on mower.

José and his wife, Blanche, are from Belgium and own a wonderful sprawling home opposite the village church. It is believed it was once a priory. José is a retired banking CEO, and he and Blanche split their time between this house that they have painstakingly restored and their home just south of Brussels.

The mystery of who had been cutting our grass here has finally been solved. He declares himself 'le fantôme de Verrue'. José always sees the best in people, an optimist with a terrific sense of humour. Laughing with him on the side of our freshly cut village path, which connects the château with the village of Verrue, we cannot imagine what a rock José will become in our efforts to bring Purnon back to life.

Who is this person, and how did he come to rest amongst the scattered stones on the floor of a partly hidden cellar?

20 JUNE

Purnon's *basse-cour* sits at the back of the *communs est* (eastern outbuilding). A long stone retaining wall separates a higher level, where the *orangerie* is perched, from the lower courtyard. The stone retaining wall is four metres high and houses nine small vaulted cellars (*caves* in French) that were probably used for storing animal feed and farm equipment when Purnon was a thriving estate. Today the wall is partly obscured by rows of cut firewood that block the entrances to many of the *caves*. A large section of the wall has collapsed completely, exposing the earth behind it, and the ceilings of several of the cellars are crumbling badly.

I've decided to move some of the wood and explore these cellars.

It takes hours to shift the decomposing wood. Eventually, I can start to force my way in. As expected, an eclectic mix of old farm gear starts to appear - cart wheels, an old bicycle, metal tools, even a huge collection of glazed terracotta pots that were used for gathering tree sap.

In one cellar, a wall has collapsed and stones litter the floor menacingly. I proceed with caution, but something odd catches my eye. I move some of the stones and uncover the head of a statue. An elegant man with an intricately carved ruff stares back at me. Who is this person, and how did he come to rest amongst the scattered stones on the floor of a partly hidden cellar? We put it aside to show Monsieur Didier on his next visit. He is baffled. He turns to a broken bust of another male figure that's come down from the *grenier*. I can see that he is keen to solve the mystery of Purnon's stone sculptures.

Clockwise from top left:
Uncovering the bust of King Henri IV in the *basse-cour* cellar.
Sunrise over the corridor that leads to our *boulangerie*.
The chapel balcony.
An oculus on the *communs est*.

23 JUNE

It seems every French village has a little *resto* called Le Cheval Blanc. Monts-sur-Guesnes in our neighbouring commune proves no exception. On a whim we pop in for lunch to check it out. But it's packed and the owner shakes his head. '*Complet.*' We're full. One of the locals calls the owner over. A discreet conversation ensues and then the owner's face lights up in a great smile. '*Eh! Vous êtes les Australiens de Purnon, non?*' Of course he can make space. A table emerges and a couple of chairs are pilfered from neighbouring tables. Everyone shuffles a little. We signal our gratitude and take our seats.

Le Cheval Blanc is run by the ever-cheerful Fredo alongside his no-nonsense wife, Christiane. Naturally, Fredo instantly becomes Fredo the frog to Flick and me (but of course never within earshot!). It's the type of cheap and cheerful *resto* that typifies rural France away from the tourist hordes. There's no menu. The courses simply start arriving almost as soon as you sit down, and they're accompanied by a carafe of bracingly honest chilled red *vin du table* that is plonked inelegantly before you. You pour the wine yourself and hang onto your cutlery for the next course as the plates are cleared. Dishes arrive, you serve yourself a portion and then the bowl or plate disappears for another table. It's crowded and loud and we love it.

Fredo's an obsessive and proud gardener. Much of what he serves is grown in his garden. We visit his home and tour his garden in a local hamlet and welcome Fredo and his wife, Christiane, at the château. They're very chuffed.

1 JULY

La Comtesse Nicole de Rochequairie is a remarkable woman. These days her home is in the former presbytery in the village. She is Pierre's aunt and lived at the château with her now-deceased husband, Jean-Pierre, in the late 1960s. She is defiant, mischievous and energetic. Although struggling a little with her eyesight and hearing, she is the keeper of the history of the modern era of the château. She patiently explains who occupied many of the rooms. Nicole owned an antique store in Paris before settling back in Verrue. She has an expert recall of the manner in which many of Purnon's rooms were decorated. Intriguing photos are brought to life as Nicole explains the personalities captured, posing in an era before saturation photography was available on every smartphone.

2 JULY

At the top of Purnon's *grand escalier*, visitors are delivered onto the first floor. It seems obvious to us, so familiar with the design of modern buildings, to expect rooms to be arranged along a corridor or hallway. But traditionally rooms in grand homes were arranged sequentially, and each room was entered by simply passing through the previous one, an arrangement known as *en enfilade* in French. The ground floor at Purnon is designed in this fashion. In the late seventeenth century, for reasons of privacy and efficiency, corridors began to be used. Purnon, constructed in the late eighteenth century, benefited from this evolution in design. The various principal bedrooms on the first floor are arranged along a wide access corridor. The rooms have high ceilings, wonderful volumes and delightful views over the *grand allée* to the north or the parc anglais to the south. They boast carefully crafted *boiseries* in Louis XVI patterns. The floor plan is complicated. The eight bedrooms on this level have more than a dozen smaller rooms attached to them. Over time many have been converted into bathrooms and toilets, but at the time of the château's construction they would have been dressing rooms and small sleeping compartments for servants.

Clockwise from top left:
José de Penaranda – immortalised in one of Purnon's
gilded frames!
A first floor bedroom.
The formidable Comtesse Nicole de Rochequairie.
The *grand salon* with its outlook over the Forêt de Scévolles.

IT SOMETIMES FEELS LIKE A JOURNEY INTO THE HEART OF DARKNESS AS THE FURTHER WE ASCEND, THE WORSE EVERYTHING BECOMES.

Through a door that leads off the *grand escalier* we can continue up to the second floor. It sometimes feels like a journey into the heart of darkness as the further we ascend, the worse everything becomes. The first floor with the principal bedrooms is not too bad – some cracked floor tiles, a few broken windowpanes, leaky pipes and just the cobwebs and dust of decades of neglect. The staircase to the second floor exhibits a disconcerting bend. Black discolouration on the walls reveals the impact of humidity. Arriving on the second floor landing is an arresting shock for first-time visitors to the château. The water leaks through the roof have caused huge damage. Massive oak beams have rotted through in places and inevitably plaster ceilings have collapsed. The wallpaper has long since peeled off and droops sadly to the floor. Broken windowpanes lay shattered on the tiles and bats fly frantically past. In winter we try not to disturb them during their hibernation. With their heart rate lowered, drawing on carefully preserved stores of energy, awakening them could have fatal consequences.

The furniture on the second floor, much of it in an advanced state of disrepair, has been rudely shoved aside to make way for every conceivable bucket and pan that we can press into service to collect water dripping from the roof above.

People often assume that the second floor was reserved for domestic staff, but its floor plan closely mirrors that of the first level. These spacious rooms with luxury wallpapers were definitely not intended for servants. Instead, it's likely that they were used for guests – perhaps for friends invited to participate in the hunting parties held in the surrounding forest.

Ascending the *grand escalier*.

The second floor is like an eighteenth-century Pompeii: time has stood still.

There is no plumbing at all on the second floor, just a single pump in one room that would have drawn water for handbasins for those staying on this level. Guests would have availed themselves of the wooden commodes with porcelain chamber-pots that we find arranged randomly around. Signs sit below various windows exhorting guests not to empty the bedpans out of the windows into the dry moat below. It's good advice. The dry moat housed herb and vegetable gardens supplying the kitchens feeding those staying at the château.

The second floor is like an eighteenth-century Pompeii: time has stood still. We find a room of huge wardrobes; the shelves still stacked with the carefully labelled linen and evening garments of the marquis and the marquise. Fireplaces full of kindling sit in darkened rooms. It seems impossible that anybody has entered some of these rooms in decades, much less slept in them. Over the months and years ahead, these rooms will gradually give up their secrets - not necessarily things of high monetary value, but the keys to unlocking some of the château's mysteries.

The marquis and marquise's linen press.

IT SEEMS IMPOSSIBLE THAT ANYBODY HAS ENTERED SOME OF THESE ROOMS IN DECADES.

Right: The once elegant furnishings of the second floor are a distant memory. Today the rooms lay abandoned and decayed.
Far right: An oculus. An eye to the decline of the second floor.

SMALL *Steps*

PETIT À PETIT, L'OISEAU FAIT SON NID.

Little by little, the bird builds its nest.
(Persevere, be patient.)

18 JULY

The grounds of most châteaux of the eighteenth century have an *orangerie*, a glasshouse for protecting citrus trees during the cold winter months. They are often buildings of immense charm, evoking antiquity with stone columns and triangular pediments. Purnon's *orangerie* lies hidden in plain sight, sitting next to the château but now completely overgrown. Like the ruins at Angkor Wat, huge trees grow inside the building and have brought down its *ardoise* roof. Large stone blocks have toppled inside and out, with traces of their intricate carvings chronicling the *orangerie*'s sad decay. So much vegetation is now suffocating the structure that we had not even realised it was there on our first visit to Purnon!

One evening, enjoying an *apéro* with José, he casually offers to help clear it. We laugh. It's a big task. Offers to help at Purnon are commonplace and we learn not to take them seriously.

'If I promise, I will come,' he says simply.

The following day, José arrives armed with his chainsaw. It is somewhat larger than mine and I immediately experience chainsaw envy. More usefully, José actually knows how to use his chainsaw. He sets to work clearing the trees around the *orangerie*. We must protect the stone structure at all costs, and José's experience in knowing exactly how to bring the trees down safely proves invaluable. I start dragging the rapidly accumulating mass of branches away. It's hard work.

After the trees are cleared, we use ladders to painstakingly remove the ivy. Protecting the stonework while working at heights is not always easy. If we pull too hard, we risk causing further damage.

As we clear the vegetation, we can gradually prise open the old iron doors into the *orangerie* itself. More trees come down with even greater care required. We start to lift the rotted roof beams that have collapsed and clear the huge quantities of broken *ardoise* tiles. It's effectively an old greenhouse, so shattered plate glass lies everywhere. We start to remove wheelbarrow-loads of soil that has accumulated over the decades since the roof's collapse.

It takes weeks. But José arrives every day – when my enthusiasm wanes in the face of this seemingly impossible task, his positive spirit and optimism keeps me going. Every château needs a José.

We unearth buried treasures: the old heating system, stone shelving, Versailles planter boxes, even the wrought iron legs of garden benches. The legs will prove vital months later on another project.

We lay all of the metal to one side. These pieces may provide the clues that will help us honour its original design. With our *orangerie* now visible, we can finally admire its ruined charm. One day we hope to restore this enchanting building.

The ruins of Ancient Rome and Greece inspired
the architectural trend that shaped our *orangerie*.

WE UNEARTH BURIED TREASURES:
THE OLD HEATING SYSTEM,
STONE SHELVING, VERSAILLES
PLANTER BOXES, EVEN
THE WROUGHT-IRON LEGS
OF GARDEN BENCHES.

The rising sun captures the beauty of Purnon's
crumbling *orangerie*.

19 JULY

Sangeetha, one of Flick's dearest friends, has arrived at Purnon.
A human rights barrister in London, she is eager to work and
clearly loves Purnon's open spaces. Each night we dine on the
back bridge that traverses the dry moat and watch the *chevreuils*
playing in the park. Two stone sphinx-like figures in an advanced
state of ruin stand sentinel flanking the end of the bridge. On
closer inspection it's apparent that they are in fact lions - flashes
of their mane are just discernible.

Together Sangeetha and Flick set to work converting a
dark *entresol* (mezzanine) room off the grand escalier into a
light-filled laundry. Flick comes across an immense enamelled
cast-iron laundry basin incongruously buried in the garden. It's
almost too heavy to lift, so we transport it to the château in the
Renault tractor and clean it out. It's in perfect condition. We buy a
washing machine and, after some electrical and plumbing work,
we no longer have to use a laundromat several towns away to
wash our clothes. We have our own laundry. It feels like luxury!

24 JULY

Monsieur Didier, our architect, has arrived for his regular visit
with exciting news: he has solved the mystery of our sculpted
busts. Careful study of nineteenth-century postcards has revealed
that the busts sat above our central dormers atop the front and
back of the château roof. Iron plinths are still visible that would
have supported these pieces of art. The north-facing bust at the
front of the château is in the likeness of King Henri IV, one of
France's most beloved rulers. The bust at the rear facing south
bears a likeness to King Louis XV. It's a great discovery. Royal
busts on châteaux that were not actually occupied by royalty are
extremely rare. Could they be restored and returned to their place
atop Purnon's magnificent roof?

Careful study of the archives has also finally revealed the
name of Purnon's original architect. He was Monsieur Bourgeoise,
based in the city of Tours. Documents at the château reveal his
daily work log. Many secrets are being unlocked. His notes record
the source of the materials used to build the château as well as
the original function of many of Purnon's various rooms.

Flick and Sangeetha relaxing on the bridge - clearing
the vegetation will soon reveal the partially hidden lions.

25 JULY

As the *grenier* quickly clears, I start to notice that several of the containers collecting the roof's leaking water are in fact nineteenth-century kitchen copperware. It's hard to believe that they have been repurposed in this way.

We start to gather the various pieces and relocate them to the original basement kitchen. The collection grows. We find some lids and on closer inspection notice they are engraved with the name de Goyon, who lived at Purnon in the 1850s. It's another remarkable discovery, possibly a wedding gift from the mid-nineteenth century. They've been at Purnon for around a hundred and seventy years.

Flick posts a photo on our growing Instagram account. A couple of days later Pierre de Rochequairie arrives, keen to eyeball our recent find. He sheepishly admits that he has several others from the set stored at La Gloriette. He's clearly a little unhappy that he didn't find them all!

It's another remarkable discovery ... they've been at Purnon for around a hundred and seventy years.

3 AUGUST

Our village is home to the workshop of local stonemason Monsieur Alain Costa. His expertise lies in heritage projects, meaning that he is qualified to work on heritage-listed buildings like those at Purnon. It's a stroke of unbelievable luck to have someone of Alain's experience and skill so close to the château.

Not surprisingly, Alain and his team are in high demand throughout the region. He finally arrives and we instantly warm to him. He has a broad smile and a slightly conspiratorial grin. He takes us on a tour of our château and shows us various projects he has completed over the years.

We lead him to our *communs est*, which house the château *boulangerie*. We've already cleared it out to reveal a sizable *four à pain* (bread oven). Can it be restored? His experienced eye appraises the oven. He even climbs inside. Yes, he finally declares. He returns a few days later with one of his crew. A few hours and the work is complete. He leaves instructions: first let the mortar set completely, then heat it slowly with the entrance blocked. He shows us where to look for telltale smoke indicating where further work is required. We burn for three days. The oven performs perfectly.

Amongst the junk we find two gigantic wooden baking peels (*pelles* in French) and an old, rusted metal dough cutter.

We order new pizza peels online and Purnon pizza nights are born.

Left: Some of the de Goyon copperware finds its home in Purnon's basement kitchen.
Following page: Purnon's *boulangerie* before the restoration of the *four à pain*.

STANDING HERE ADMIRING OUR
WORK ON PURNON'S WINE CELLAR
MAKES ME MISS HIM PAINFULLY.
I HOPE THAT HE IS SOMEWHERE
SHARING IN OUR ADVENTURE.

4 AUGUST

The summer heat brings invasions of nesting wasps (*guêpes*). They pack a vicious sting, as I discover when I lift the lid on the pool filter to inspect its condition.

We fashion rudimentary traps from recycled plastic bottles laced with honey and beer (what a waste!) and suspend them in trees. It's not very effective, so Sangeetha and I set to work hunting for the nests. We follow at dusk when they are active, and before long we spot a series of large nests perched in the upper reaches of our *grenier* and in some of the damaged stonework on the exterior of the château. We start by suspending our traps directly in front of the nests. But then impatience overtakes us, and a few days later we're attacking the nests with wasp spray and then smashing them with poles. We deserve to be savagely attacked by swarms of angry wasps. But we're lucky and the danger abates.

21 AUGUST

My birthday! Flick has manufactured elegant wine tags out of the *ardoise* tiles from Purnon's roof. Sangeetha has organised a wine tour and tasting at a Chinon winery. It's a welcome break from work for the three of us.

My dad loved a great wine cellar. In every home he and Mum lived in, Dad found ingenious ways to create a space to store and enjoy his wine. It reached peak folly when he built an English pub under their home in Melbourne and proceeded to entertain guests there. And they say the apple doesn't fall far from the tree!

Purnon's *cave à vin* (wine cellar) extends over three rooms, with storage racks for thousands of bottles. But it's in a terrible state. Rotting shelves attest to the cellar's humidity. Junk is everywhere. Some of it is old and might be worth saving - barrels and vintage bottles. Most of it is rubbish - discarded bottles, cardboard boxes, broken glass.

Several tonnes of excess soil and sand have been dumped there, raising the floor level and adding to the chaos. We set to work moving wheelbarrow-loads of earth out into our dry moat. Shifting the soil uncovers twenty-four old bottles of unlabelled red wine buried beneath the surface. And then the marquis' own slate wine tags start to appear, buried underground. They date back to the beginning of the nineteenth century - we spot Châteauneuf-du-Pape and Bordeaux from 1810.

We put down a loose white gravel floor - a couple of hundred twenty-kilogram bags that we must bring in by hand through the tunnels that connect the *douve sèche* (dry moat) to the closest point we can reach with our trailer. It's back-breaking work. Then a large custom-made table supported by oak Bordeaux wine barrels arrives. Other barrels acquired from a local winery serve as smaller degustation tables. Our wine collection starts to grow, occupying the marquis' old metal racks. Flick's wine labels look amazing.

My father was a rock in so many of my life's milestones. Standing here admiring our work on Purnon's wine cellar makes me miss him painfully. I hope that he is somewhere sharing in our adventure.

20 SEPTEMBER

It's *les journées du patrimoine*. Each year, historic buildings across France, many of them normally off limits to the public, open free of charge to give local people a chance to see their own heritage up close. Due to its advanced state of disrepair, Purnon had never been opened in such a way.

As soon as we arrived and realised the château's significance to the life of the local community, we were determined that her doors should be thrown open for people to get an *avant-goût* (preview) before scaffolding and building works started her transformation.

We register our intention to open with the region's online database and our architect generously agrees to speak to an assembled throng in the afternoon to describe our proposed restoration.

Mayor Francis Siclet and his team of deputies swing into action. Posters around the village spread the word and the hardworking team from the commune depot help cut hedges and paths to provide access for visitors. I was surprised when one of the municipal workers stopped his tractor on our front prairie and began taking photos of the château. He told me he'd lived in Verrue all his life and his mother had worked at Purnon but he had never been inside the domain walls. I was shocked and touched at how emotional he appeared.

The day finally arrives and we expect a modest crowd of curious locals.

The horde builds quickly, despite the morning rain. Soon the prairie we're using as a car park is overwhelmed and a traffic jam (wonderfully named a *bouchon* or 'cork' in French) snakes through the village. Verrue has never seen anything like it. People queue patiently at the front of the château to view the grand salon. The national newspaper Le Monde has listed Purnon as one of the top ten attractions across France for this year's *journées du patrimoine*. It is the only attraction listed outside the greater Paris area.

It proves an emotional day – people arrive clutching historic postcards of the château and with fading photos of loved ones in the château grounds taken decades ago. Many visitors have a personal connection, a relative who worked or lived here. Some are seeing Purnon for the first time, others are returning after decades away.

Local members of parliament arrive.

By the afternoon, the rain has cleared and Monsieur Didier addresses over five hundred people assembled on the *cour d'honneur*. He holds them spellbound for an hour while he recounts the history of the château and its architectural peculiarities. I try to imagine such a crowd willing to listen to a technical discourse about a dilapidated private home in Australia.

Exhausted at the end of the day, we realise that over a thousand people have visited Purnon. We are beginning to understand the national significance of the building for which we are the custodians.

People arrive clutching historic postcards of the château and with fading photos of loved ones in the château grounds taken decades ago.

The restoration effort is softened by Purnon's beauty.

As we comprehend the reality that we will face winter with our roof still in its fragile and leaky state, we are starting to understand the complexity and care required to properly protect and restore a building of such importance.

The *communs est* – home to garages and our *boulangerie*.

2 OCTOBER

We meet today with our architect, Monsieur Didier, and the representatives of the French government who will oversee the work to restore Purnon. Based in Poitiers, they are from the Direction Régionale des Affaires Culturelles (DRAC). The team with whom we will work is led by the enthusiastic and supportive Madame Agathe Bordeau.

Their involvement is vital as the château (both inside and out), the two *communs*, the *cour d'honneur*, the terraces, the *douve* and the 1812 gate are all *classé* (listed), while the Moulin Bigeard, Éolienne Bollée and potager garden with its charming pavilion are *inscrit* (registered, a slightly lesser form of protection). The most architecturally or historically significant buildings in France are either *classé* or *inscrit* as *monuments historiques*. This system is designed to catalogue the world's most extraordinary collection of built heritage. It also provides for its legal protection and helps organise public and private funds to preserve this national patrimony.

Saving Purnon is well beyond the financial resources of Flick and me. Recognising the importance of leveraging private funds to secure the protection of the vast number of listed buildings, the French government provides public funds for a percentage of the cost of the works. It's a complicated and opaque process. Understandably, they only fund those portions of a property that are listed (forget about getting your pool or modern kitchen installed with a contribution from the French taxpayer!).

My mind drifts back to Australian politics, and I wonder how Australian taxpayers would feel about public money funding the restoration of private homes often in the hands of well-off foreigners. But without this government support, our project would be impossible and the value of our private investment would be lost.

Flick and I are confronting the sobering truth that the huge works to save Purnon will not start immediately. Months of careful study are required to plan the immense project. Every element of the building needs to be assessed and understood before a plan can be prepared to execute its restoration.

As we comprehend the reality that we will face winter with our roof still in its fragile and leaky state, we are starting to understand the complexity and care required to properly protect and restore a building of such importance.

The first and most urgent works to save Château de Purnon will be the roof and stone façades of the château itself. These will form stage one, and it will be the most important (and expensive!) stage of the works. Madame Bordeau brings the welcome news that DRAC has agreed to support sixty per cent of the cost of the stage one works. With these works already forecast to cost just over two million euros, we are hugely grateful – it's the maximum level of funding that DRAC can provide.

We had met with the DRAC team prior to signing the contracts to purchase Purnon, when they had undertaken to support the château's restoration. Now that the restoration project is a reality, it's a massive relief to know that DRAC will accompany us on our difficult journey.

18 OCTOBER

Chasing hunting dogs out of the domain, I chance upon an extraordinary discovery.

On the edge of our woods I come across some corrugated iron sheeting. I move it aside to reveal a massive stone well. It's clearly very old and some distance from our buildings. Perhaps it is a hint to the layout of an earlier château, which occupied the domain centuries ago.

It astounds us that we are still making new discoveries six months after our arrival.

1 NOVEMBER

It's *la Toussaint* (All Saints' Day) and in Catholic France chrysanthemums are typically laid on relatives' tombs. The Verrue cemetery is deserted, and we place some flowers on the de Rochequairie plot before wandering around the small but well-maintained grounds, finding the resting places of family members of some of the people we've met in the short time since we arrived. As well as de Rochequairies we spot Siclets, Pelletiers and Autins. We even find a plot for a Monsieur Firmin Auguste Courdonneau whose headstone records him as 'Piqueur du Château de Purnon' for what appears to be an incredible sixty years during the nineteenth century. The *piqueur* is a valet who leads the hounds on the hunt.

But there is no sign of Purnon's original owners, the Achard de la Haye family, and at the recent *journées du patrimoine*, someone had insisted that they too were interred here.

My curiosity is aroused. I visit the *mairie* (town hall) in the village, which doubles as a post office. Véronique produces a folder containing the records of the cemetery. A map marks all the plots and there are some old handwritten notes. Sure enough, Antoine-Charles, his wife, Bénigne-Modeste, their son Édouard (mayor of Verrue from 1800 to 1830) and even Pauline de Goyon are recorded on plots numbered from eighty to eighty-six. The inscriptions on the headstones have long since worn away.

Clockwise from top left:
Chamber pots and bidets from the unplumbed second floor.
A package for the Comte de Lézardière, who was married
at Purnon just before the First World War.
Some of the abandoned books from the library at Purnon.
A glimpse of the second floor.

8 NOVEMBER

Our first autumn at Purnon and we are struck by the incredible colour. The park turns into a sea of gold, brown and yellow. The days are still long and warm and the sky clear.

And then, suddenly, the leaves fall and our paths disappear under a thick crackling carpet. As the autumn sun sets behind the Éolienne Bollée, the sky glows an incredible red.

9 NOVEMBER

The Moulin Bigeard is a sprawling farmhouse. Built around the middle of the seventeenth century, it's the oldest building on the estate. Although in a terrible state, it has some charming features, including an old *four à pain*. José and I have set to work clearing a walled garden at the back of the *moulin*.

José carefully fells dozens of trees that have turned the yard into a jungle. I remove overgrown wire fences and much of the undergrowth and we begin clearing masses of rubbish. It takes a couple of weeks of hard physical labour. The kilograms start to fall off me. Soon I weigh less than I did in my twenties.

We move on to clear the base around the nearby *pigeonnier*. Our semi-ruined *pigeonnier* is a fascinating reminder of pre-revolutionary France. Keeping pigeons was a feudal right connected with the amount of land a noble family owned, but the pigeons inevitably ravaged the seeds sowed by impoverished local tenant farmers. This formed one of the many grievances that led eventually to revolution. Sadly, the wall on one side of ours has collapsed. By cutting back the trees that are slowly strangling her, we hope we can at least prevent further damage. We can see the *boulins*, the little niches where pairs of pigeons would have lived and mated. Beneath the *boulins*, the pigeon waste was collected as fertiliser.

Inside the walled garden itself, a late-nineteenth-century *serre* (glasshouse) occupies one side of the yard. Like the *orangerie*, trees are growing right through it. José sets to work with the chainsaw and soon the worst trees have been felled. Alain Costa, our stonemason, arrives, curious to see what we are up to. He spots the danger that one of largest trees poses to the stonework of the *serre* and calls in one of his best workers, Frédéric. Despite Frédéric's large frame, he nimbly mounts the shaky ladder resting on the side of the *serre*, eschewing the safety helmet that José proffers. He's standing on a narrow, crumbling stone ledge without a safety rope in sight. As a former minister for workplace safety, I try to look away. The chainsaw kicks into life and he expertly attacks the tree from the precise angle and height required, and the upper part of the tree falls with no damage to the *serre*. From ground level, cutting the base of the trunk will now be easy. More importantly, Frédéric descends safely to earth.

With the trees and undergrowth cleared, the walled garden looks fabulous. Flick arrives with a late afternoon *apéro* as the sun sets against a beautiful autumnal blue sky. We warm ourselves by the bonfire that consumes much of what we have cleared.

OUR SEMI-RUINED PIGEONNIER IS A FASCINATING REMINDER OF PRE-REVOLUTIONARY FRANCE.

Previous page: The seventeenth-century Moulin Bigeard
Right: Flick and I ponder our semi-ruined *pigeonnier*
with the *boulins* clearly visible.

The *serre* or glasshouse occupies part of the walled
garden behind the Moulin Bigeard.

At Purnon we spend a lot of time thinking about the past. Yet when I see Purnon's books casually stacked in dusty piles, I instead ponder the future.

Just some of the thousands of books that lay scattered through the *bibliothèque* when we first arrived.

15 NOVEMBER

At Purnon we spend a lot of time thinking about the past. Yet when I see Purnon's books casually stacked in dusty piles, I instead ponder the future. Will we really one day live in a world without hardcopy books? What will we have lost when that day arrives?

Wedged inside a discarded book stacked haphazardly in the *bibliothèque*, I come across a handwritten inventory dated 1854. It is a carefully prepared list detailing all of the books contained in Purnon's library in the mid-nineteenth century and lists over a thousand volumes. Almost none remain.

But the handwritten inventory is wonderful. The elaborate calligraphy of the era reveals a complete history of France, the Wars of Religion, the eighteenth century, the French Revolution and the Restoration. The works of many great writers - Fontaine, Chateaubriand, Walter Scott, Voltaire, Racine - are represented. Of course, the great writers to come - Victor Hugo, Jules Verne, Balzac - are absent. The collection displays an obsession with the lives of French kings and chivalrous orders that is completely comprehensible in families of ardent royalists.

It's easy to believe that a grand book collection is a fading memory. For the owners of Purnon, the sum of human knowledge would have been carefully arranged in the tomes stacked along the shelves of the *bibliothèque*. Today, technology has made the book redundant as the great repository of knowledge. If we want to know something, we can just google it.

Old books are objects of such sensory beauty - the way they look, feel and smell. But what will we lose if we allow books to transition merely to things of elegance and prestige, an objet d'art like a painting or a print or a clock?

The internet takes us immediately and abruptly to our intended destination. Whereas to admire a collection of books and select from its contents draws you down unexpected tracks, hidden pathways and random wanderings. A book is an invitation to stop and sit down, to admire the writer's craft and not just the information conveyed.

We've been collecting antiquarian books for years. Soon it will be our collection that graces the bookcases that will adorn the *bibliothèque* at Purnon. Our friends will be able to inhale the sensory delight of old books, randomly select something unexpected from the collection and while away a few hours turning its pages.

WHEN WE ACQUIRED THE CHÂTEAU, THE FAMILY ABANDONED AN IMPRESSIVE ÉRARD GRAND PIANO.

24 NOVEMBER

Clearing the woods at the back of the *orangerie*, I chance upon a disturbing discovery: a thirty-centimetre-long unexploded anti-aircraft shell. We've been warned by the *gendarmerie* (military police force) that old military ordinance is a hazard in France and call them as instructed. The bomb squad is dispatched from La Rochelle to collect it and they identify it as a practice round. I'm secretly a little disappointed.

27 NOVEMBER

Flick's birthday. She must follow the rhyming clues to some of our favourite places around Purnon. We end in the *cave à vin* for a tasting plate and a glass of red. Her gift is a *montgolfière* (hot air balloon) ride that will depart from the *cour d'honneur* when the weather is better. Let's be honest, it's as much a gift for me!

10 DECEMBER

When we acquired the château, the family abandoned an impressive Érard grand piano. A thoughtful birthday gift from Flick's siblings sees a piano tuner dispatched to see if it can be tuned.

Soon the château echoes with Elton John's 'Song for Guy'. It's starting to feel like a home. But the wing of the château housing the piano is arctic. The local Christmas market at Mont-sur-Guesnes peddles fingerless gloves so that Flick can practise.

Previous page left to right:
Flick doesn't seem too perturbed entering one of the many tunnels that connect several of Purnon's buildings.
The tack rooms. Horses were once part of daily life at Purnon. Flick dreams of bringing them back.
Right: The Érard grand piano, tuned for the first time in decades.

15 DECEMBER

Sangliers (wild boar) are destroying our paddocks. These animals can wreak enormous havoc in just one night. Worse, they appear to be damaging our neighbouring farmers' pastures, using their massive heads to plough the earth. They are going to have to be dealt with.

The *sangliers* stamp a less than subtle path through our *bois* (woods) and prairie. It should make tracking them easy.

But *sangliers* are not to be trifled with – they are enormously strong beasts and can run surprisingly fast. We are assured that they can even jump. Their protruding canine teeth can cause horrific injuries.

On the appointed day, Monsieur Costa arrives with a team to hunt them down. As well as being an expert stonemason, he's also handy with a firearm.

It's a well-organised operation. After acquiring the scent, the dogs will drive the *sangliers* north towards the forest. The *garde de la chasse* (effectively, the chief of the hunt) sports a brass horn slung across his torso. Armed men form a line along the forest edge, while the dogs and other hunters drive the *sangliers* forward. Shots ring out. Six have been killed.

Hours later, the team returns to Purnon. Flick is presented with a large bag containing bloody hunks of red meat. We try to be polite, but her distaste is obvious. They depart and return the next day with the meat expertly butchered. We prepare a *sanglier* stew. With lashings of paprika and cooked for hours on our stove, it is superb. I feel a guilty pleasure feasting on something that caused so much damage to our fields.

19 DECEMBER

We've sold the International tractor. It was proving too temperamental in my unskilled hands. A canny local farmer will no doubt make her sing. I need to start freeing up garage space for modern equipment more suitable for maintaining the château grounds rather than the hundreds of hectares of surrounding farmland that formed part of the original estate.

20 DECEMBER

A trip to Emmaus (the French equivalent of an op shop) in Poitiers and Flick and I have bought two second-hand bikes as our Christmas presents for one another. It's a pretty frugal gift, but it was fun searching through the bargain treasures.

We came across a nineteenth-century French edition of *Robinson Crusoe*. It matches exactly an English edition I found for Flick several years ago in Melbourne.

Daniel Defoe based the central character on the real-life castaway Alexander Selkirk, of whom Flick is a descendent. It's a great story, and as bibliophiles we're always looking to add to the collection of memorabilia.

25 DECEMBER

It's Christmas Day and we play host to José and Blanche for lunch. Flick has decorated the table spectacularly. Our *salle à manger* comes alive for formal events like this. It's wonderful to enjoy José's company without the threat of a chainsaw coughing into life!

31 DECEMBER

Flick's friends Kristin, Adrian and Eve are our guests for New Year's Eve. The *sanglier* stew makes another appearance. While it slowly cooks, we regale them with stories of how it was hunted. You'd think I'd shot it myself. But we've boasted too soon – the gas bottles cut out and I spend a nervous half hour outside in the dark trying to make our old cooktop gas supply restart. Finally, it works.

A magnificent electrical storm appears to the north. The lightning turns the night into day, illuminating us eerily as we sit perched in Purnon's giant windows, wineglasses in hand, watching nature's show.

The basement with its vaulted stone ceilings.

THE Darkness
BEFORE THE DAWN

LA MAYONNAISE NE PREND PAS.

The mayonnaise isn't taking.
(Things take an unfavourable turn.)

1 JANUARY

A new year and we are a bit slow starting. Working almost every day since arriving in May is starting to take its toll physically. It couldn't possibly be the wine. In the late afternoon, we clear sections of nearby woods and make a large bonfire. Kristin, Adrian and Eve pitch in and we get a lot done. The warmth of the fire proves perfect for an *apéro* as the sun quickly disappears. In its warm glow, Flick and I resolve to try to spend more time enjoying our home in the new year. With so much that we hope to achieve, perhaps it's a naive aspiration.

7 JANUARY

In my spare moments, I've been working on Purnon's *glacière*. It's the eighteenth century's answer to the deep freezer.

Usually, a large hole was excavated into a small hillock or directly into the ground. It was lined with stone and normally had some kind of domed top. During winter, successive layers of snow and straw were packed in and meat and fish stored frozen in the centre.

Purnon's *glacière* lies hidden in the woods hundreds of metres from the château. Unbelievably, successive generations have used it as a rubbish dump. The roof has long since collapsed. We've started the terrible task of extracting decades of waste and separating it for recycling - glass, plastic, metal and shoes ... extraordinary quantities of shoes. With a shovel, it's a thankless and impossible task. There must be a better way!

11 JANUARY

When we purchased Purnon, one of the unresolved issues was the fate of the incredible château archives. Huge wooden chests hold the records of the Achard de la Haye family going back many centuries. The oldest are written on animal-skin parchments (in some cases vellum) and inscribed in remarkable classical French. The documents include correspondence, bail agreements, cadastral maps and even census records from periods when family members served as local mayors. Several documents carry the wax royal seal of King Louis XVI. The archives also include boxes of documents from the de Rochequairie family extending well into the twentieth century.

For us, the documents are a blessing and a curse. They obviously contain material vital to understanding the history of the château. But some are incredibly fragile and already displaying serious signs of decay. They are disorganised and intermingled with records from other properties. Protecting and curating them is a task completely beyond our capacity.

Negotiations over their purchase quickly broke down and the de Rochequairie family instead sold them to the archives section of the department of Vienne. This public entity has the expertise and the facilities to restore and protect these incomparable historic records.

Mademoiselle
Mademoiselle Achard
par
Mirebeau

Louis par la grace de Dieu Roy de France et de Navarre
Louis
Par Le Roy

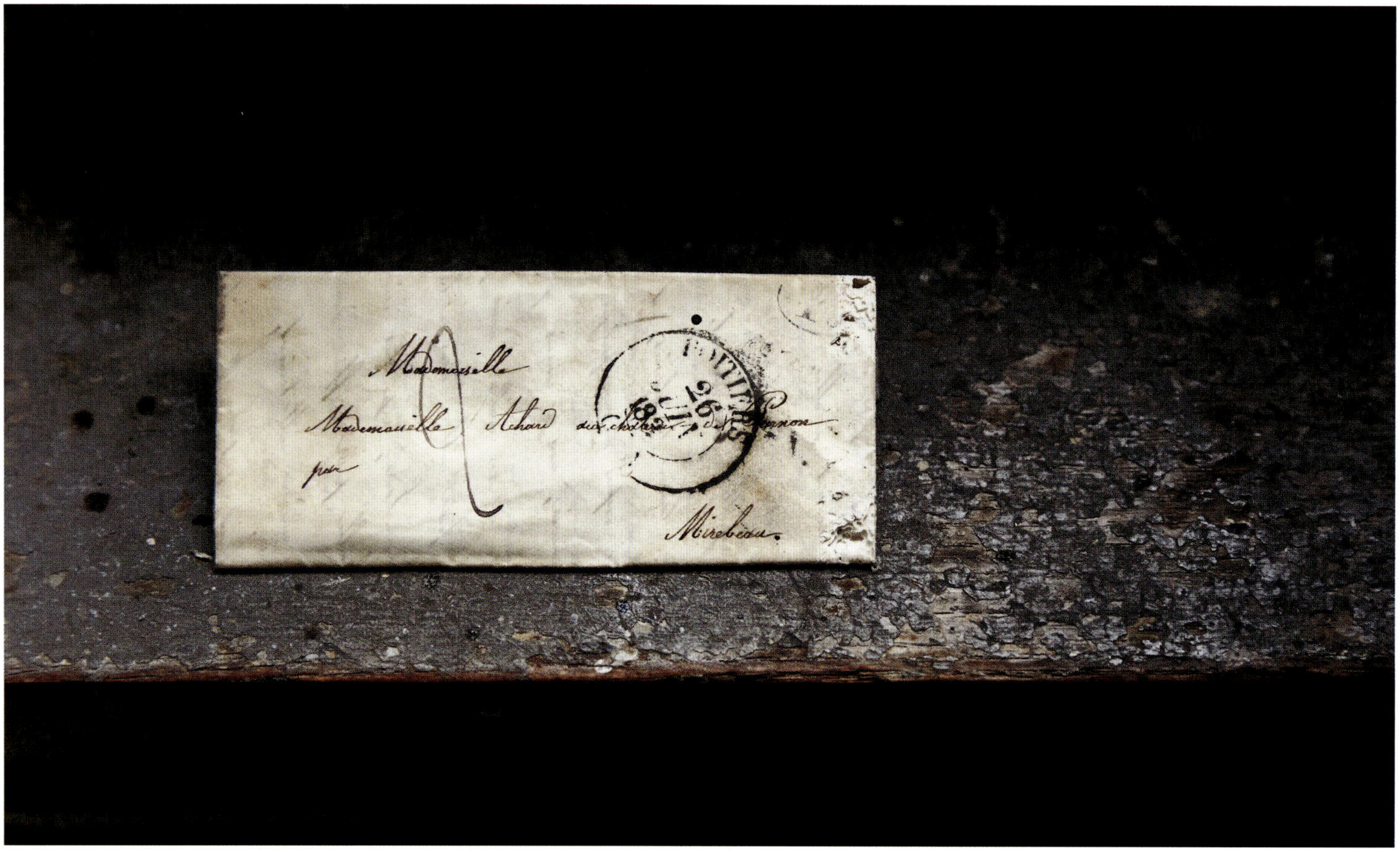

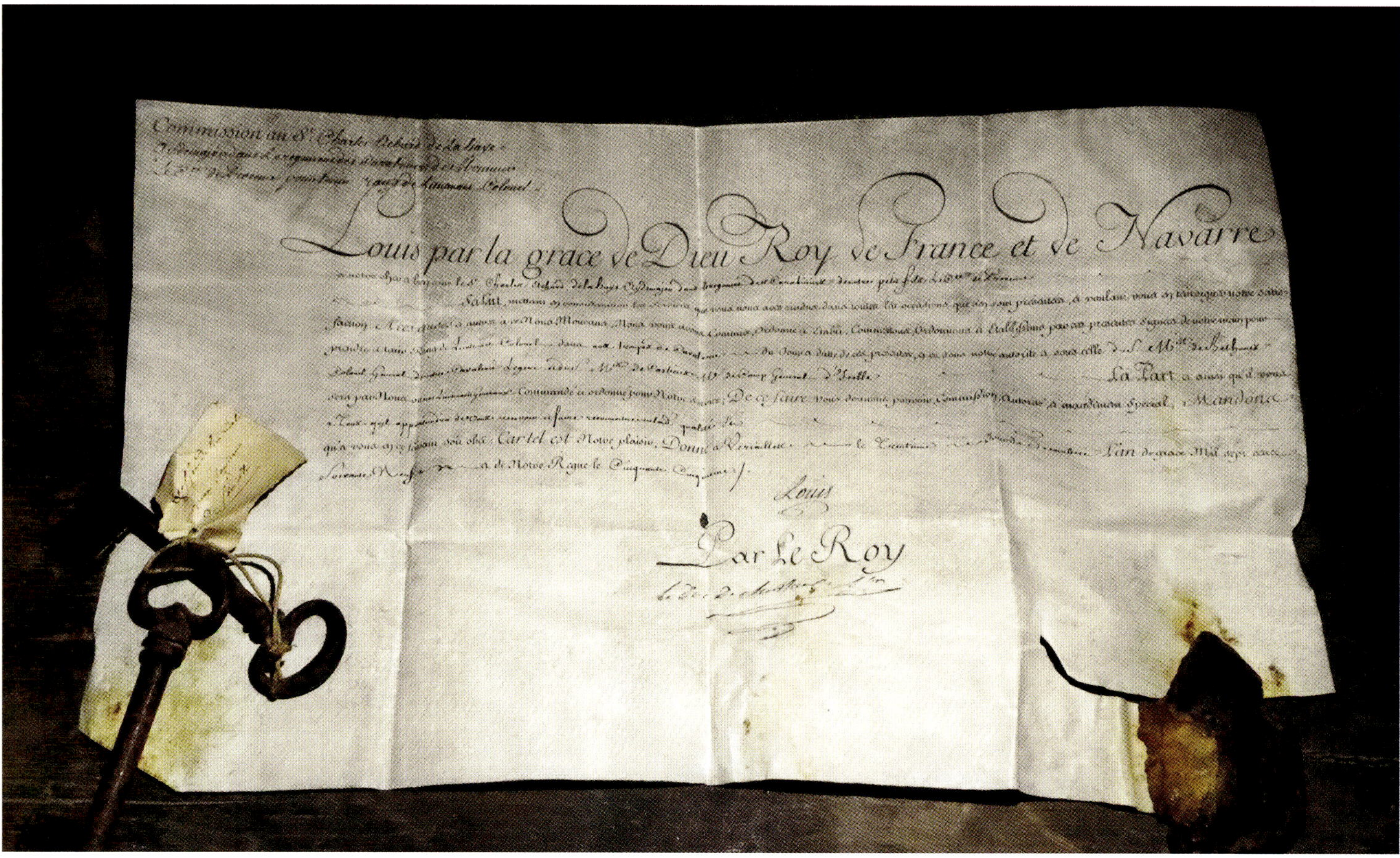

Eventually, they will be digitised and available for public access. Despite our disappointment that they are leaving Purnon, it is a better outcome than allowing them to decay in the attic.

Last year, Monsieur Didier dispatched a team to identify and copy any documents that appear relevant to the construction of the château. Much important information was extracted from this exercise and we are presented with a CD containing copies of hundreds of the documents. They include original floor plans as well as intricate designs for the façades.

Nevertheless, it's a bittersweet day as the departmental team arrives to remove the archives forever.

15 JANUARY

Rummaging around under the crooked staircase that leads to the second floor, we come across mountains of old children's shoes. I wedge myself into the uncomfortable space and begin systematically clearing them out. There are hundreds, and I sort them into pairs. A visiting neighbour arrives and is puzzled to see them carefully arranged in our *entrée* awaiting a decision about their final fate.

We explain where we found them. He is horrified. 'No!' he exclaims. 'You must return them. They are warding off evil spirits.' It's hard to conceal our scepticism at this improbable revelation. But it turns out he's quite right. It was a common practice to conceal shoes in building cavities, under stairs and even in chimneys to keep demons away. Apparently children's shoes were particularly effective. We shrug our shoulders and return them under the staircase.

I move a loose panel of wood and find a secret stash of intimate letters from the 1830s.

25 JANUARY

When the weather comes in or the sun goes down and our work around the château stops, we turn to researching the history of Purnon. We start with objects and documents that we find as we open boxes and clean out cupboards. At the back of one cupboard in the small bureau off the *salon d'hiver*, I move a loose panel of wood and find a secret stash of intimate letters from the 1830s.

We prise open a drawer of a long-forgotten secretaire on the second floor. Lying inside are a series of German newspapers from June 1940. Replete with headlines boasting of German victories and photos of Adolf Hitler receiving the French surrender in the rail carriage at Compiègne, they enable us to identify the exact days when the Germans occupied the château.

From old photos and postcards we spot features of the château that time has gradually eroded. It was from an old nineteenth-century postcard that our architect solved the mystery of the location of the broken royal busts.

We relentlessly question those still living who stayed or worked here at Purnon.

A surprising resource is provided by the immense treasure trove of information that is now accessible online. Genealogy records enable us to build highly detailed family trees. Many of these reveal births, deaths and marriages that occurred at the château. France's online military records are extraordinary. Conscription records can be searched by department. With full names we find the service records of family members using regimental histories that I spotted amongst piles of old books in the *bibliothèque*.

By far the best resource is held by the Bibliothèque national de France (BnF). Its online Gallica platform has an incomparable collection of photos, newspapers (with text search capability), magazines and even the records of historical societies and personal diaries that are held by the BnF. With patience, we start to find newspaper descriptions of Purnon weddings, including lists of notable attendees and even the gifts borne by the guests. We find a photo of our *pigeonnier* from the 1940s before it collapsed. And we come across a moving obituary to a priest at Purnon who was confessor to the de Goyon family for fifty-one years.

Restoring the château structurally is a project of immense importance. But a vital element of our journey lies in uncovering the stories of the people who lived and worked here.

Previous page: When he signed this preliminary design of the château's façade in 1781, the architect provided the vital clue to revealing his identity more than 240 years later. The restoration and protection of these fragile documents from the château archives is now the responsibility of the French government.
Top left: One of the dozens of letters discovered hidden behind a cupboard wall in the bureau.
Bottom left: An extraordinary handwritten letter from Purnon's archives carrying the wax seal and signature of King Louis XVI.

11 FEBRUARY

It's snowing! Flick and I were both working outside when in the majestic silence we realised snow was descending all around us. We called out to each other like excited children. Work was suspended for a few hours as we seized the opportunity to capture photos of the château in the fading afternoon light under a soft dusting of snowflakes.

Far left: The château under a dusting of snow.
Left: The terrace deer rests calmly under the snowflakes.

15 FEBRUARY

We're learning to value small acts of vandalism.

While Purnon's history is filled with the names of nobles who lived and sometimes died here, it's easy to imagine that the names of the people who worked in hidden parts of the château have been lost to us forever. In truth, their names are all around us.

In the *grenier*, the names of craftsmen who built and maintained the incredible roof are etched into the stone supports. The men recorded the dates of their repairs and traced the hammers that mark their trade. Some are fathers and sons - either working together or a generation apart. Occasionally visitors spot a relative's name who worked at the château many years ago.

In our *monte-plats*, the service pulley that lifted warm dishes from the basement to the dining room prior to serving, the ladies who worked in the kitchen recorded their names hidden inside its walls. The names and dates are clearly legible. As if to deliberately undermine the social observation I'm making, some unhelpful wit has etched alongside '*Les noms des hommes célèbres sont dans les livres, celui des imbeciles sur les murs*' (the names of the famous are found in books, those of idiots are on the walls). Thanks.

A young Italian refugee who stayed at Purnon during the war scratched his name into the stone on the *communs est*. It takes a visitor who recalled the boy to identify it for us. The current generation of the de Rochequairie family are surprised to learn the long-forgotten story of a boy who found shelter in their home during Europe's darkest days.

It's easy to imagine that the names of the people who worked in hidden parts of the château have been lost to us forever. In truth, their names are all around us.

Their names are not forgotten to us - graffiti leaves traces of those who worked on Purnon throughout the centuries.

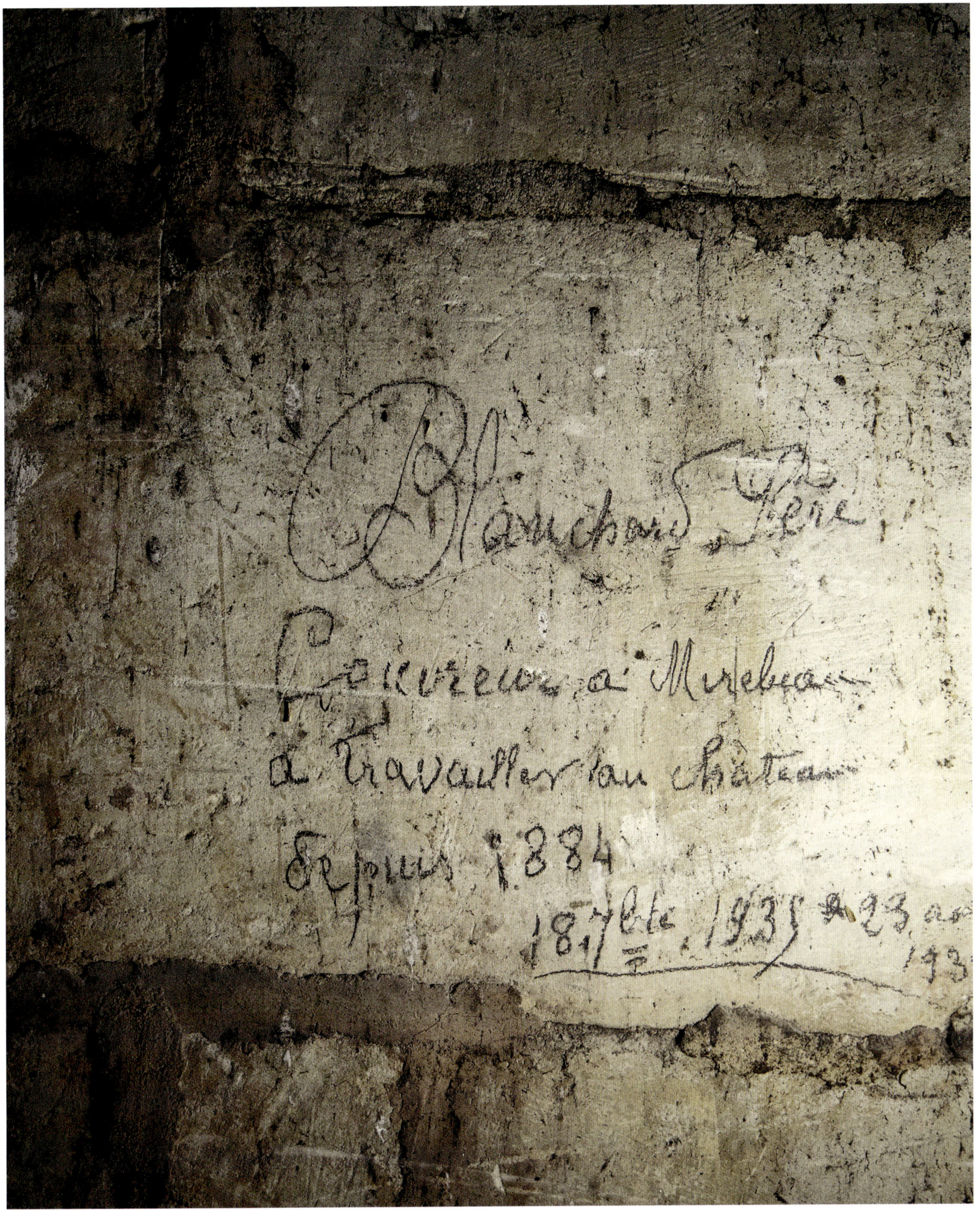
Blanchard Père,
couvreur a Mirebeau
a travailler au château
depuis 1884
18 7bre 1935 23 ao
193

ONE OF PURNON'S JEWELS IS ITS CHAPEL.

26 MARCH

One of Purnon's jewels is its chapel housed in our fragile *communs ouest* (western outbuilding). Its ceilings reach to more than seven metres. Two grand statues portray Saint Blaise (a saint venerated by farmers) and Saint Achard (the patron saint of the family that built the château). Exquisite stained-glass windows portray Saint Joseph and the Virgin and child. A magnificent depiction of the Annunciation sits above the altar. It's a huge painting of rare quality but in need of serious restoration. A slightly more modern canvas depicts Christ's descent from the Cross and graces the eastern side of the chapel. Hymn books lie scattered and an enormous confessional booth occupies one corner. I wonder if it will ever be used again. In politics I was better at pointing out the sins of others rather than admitting to my own.

But the chapel's collapsing ceiling reminds us that this will be no easy restoration. First we must relocate the artworks to prevent any damage when we eventually set to work on the roof and ceiling.

Today, the delicate task of bringing down the statues falls to Monsieur Costa's team. Scaffolding allows them a closer inspection, revealing they are made of stone, not plaster as initially thought. Good news for us. But they probably weigh over three hundred kilograms each. Access holes are created through the ceiling above, allowing support harnesses to be lowered from the outbuilding's attic. Having seen the state of that section of attic floor, it's not a task for the faint-hearted.

As each statue is carefully dislodged and then lowered, our hearts race. If they fall, they will be lost forever and the marble floor will be seriously damaged.

The operation is a success and we breathe a huge sigh of relief. The statues can be carefully cleaned and stored. But gazing at the chapel itself, we return quickly to earth. Clearing the rubble from the floor, restoring the roof and stabilising the building will be an immense task.

Left: Purnon's graceful chapel.
Following page: A good day's work – the saints are protected.

27 MARCH

We have been gradually uncovering Purnon's huge network of stone gutters.

When the château was constructed, the plastic, aluminium or zinc guttering that is today placed at roof level did not exist. Rainwater ran off the roofline and fell directly onto the ground below. Over time, prolonged rainfall could severely undermine a building's foundations.

So at Purnon, gutters comprising thousands of carefully angled and arranged stone pieces laid at ground level channelled excess rainwater into the château's drainage system. Hundreds of metres of these stone gutters sit at the base of many of our buildings. But over the years they have been covered by layers of soil and grass so thick that it takes serious spadework just to locate them. We started in the *basse-cour* and have proceeded to the front of the *communs est*. It's exhausting work, but gradually the network is beginning to emerge.

All three of us at work uncovering Purnon's network of stone gutters.

30 MARCH

Our dream to drift gently above Purnon and admire her with the birds takes shape before the sun rises.

In French it's a *montgolfière*, named after the two brothers, Joseph-Michel and Jacques-Étienne Montgolfier, who invented it. Of course, in English it is a hot air balloon. Heaven forbid the English be compelled to formally acknowledge French innovation! The Anglo-French rivalry never ceases to amuse us.

The *montgolfière* crew arrive at Purnon well before the sun to begin preparations for Flick's much delayed birthday present.

Before our eyes, the immense balloon fills. We scramble into the basket. A few short bursts of the burner and we're ascending from the *cour d'honneur.*

The château disappears beneath us. And then, in perfect silence, we are drifting over the Forêt de Scévolles, just above the treetops. It's early spring and the leaves have not yet returned. We can clearly see the forest floor and start to spot animals – *chevreuils* and *cerfs* (stags). The silence is punctuated only by the occasional bark of a dog. We whisper excitedly to one another, as if afraid that we might wake someone below. We spot hamlets, villages and other landmarks that we recognise. The breeze takes us slowly north to Loudun. As we drift over the historic town, astonished children wave eagerly at us from a schoolyard.

And then, all too quickly, it's over. We land on a thankfully deserted stretch of roadway and are dropped back at Purnon, where we bid farewell to the friendly team from Montgolfière Sensation. As they disappear down the drive, I reach for the château key. After a few panicked moments, it dawns on me that I've dropped it somewhere between climbing into the wicker basket and clambering out at the end. Our spare is rather unhelpfully with Pierre de Rochequairie and he's in Paris. A quick call to the team in the truck. And eureka! They've found it perched in the basket.

Hours later, we're still buzzing. I congratulate myself smugly on such a thoughtful birthday gift for Flick.

31 MARCH

José and I have decided to tackle the restoration of a collection of nineteenth-century garden benches.

Seven of them were extracted from the balcony of the chapel where they had been haphazardly stored. The legs of an eighth were unearthed from the *orangerie* during our excavations last year.

Each has a pair of wrought-iron legs, though some are broken and cannot be saved. The seats themselves are wooden slats, many of which prove very degraded. The screws are rusted and all will need to be replaced.

We triage the various elements and calculate that we can restore five.

We start by cleaning the legs with iron brushes. It's thankless work and not very effective. Alain Costa drops past and takes pity on us. He suggests high-pressure sandblasting and whisks them away, returning the following day. They look brand new.

In the meantime, José and I have set to work on the slats. First they need to be sanded and the old screw holes filled, then given two coats of the paint we've selected. We also paint the newly cleaned legs and a central metal brace. When everything is dry, we can start reassembling them. They look fabulous. The final touch sees the return of their original white enamel brand plates.

We've discovered a very old photo of the château terrace. We spot one of the benches facing back towards the château. It's very satisfying to return them after probably a century.

Left: The garden benches return home.
Right: Life and love at Purnon more than a century ago.
This photo inspired the restoration of our collection
of garden benches.

Left: The welcome arrival of spring.
Following page: Like the sunflowers, we celebrate
the summer sun.

11 APRIL

After the long cold winter, spring brings the château park to life. The white snowdrops (*perce-neige*) flower first and then the daffodil buds (*jonquilles*) appear, and soon the prairie is a vast carpet of yellow. Our plum trees blossom white. As the yellow daffodils wilt, they are replaced by white narcissus daffodils with six petals and a pink corona. And then the purples of lilacs (*lilas*) and hyacinths (*jacinthes*) appear. Finally come roses in an array of colours - red, yellow, white and orange. We can hear the distinctive sounds of birds all around us, including woodpeckers and cuckoos.

The days start to lengthen, slowly at first, and then by the changing of the clock it starts to feel like summer has arrived.

The farmers' fields - ploughed and seeded in the cold months - now reveal their bounty. Rotation means each year brings surprises. The *colza* (rapeseed) flowers early, creating a brilliant yellow carpet. Our favourite are the fields of incomparable sunflowers extending towards the horizon in the brightest yellow. The French name them *tournesols*, reminding us that the field of flowers will turn to best capture the sun's rays. It's an evocative name for an extraordinary flower.

Other fields boast corn and, specialties of our area, asparagus and melons. This being France, grapevines are ubiquitous, but the cabernet franc will make us wait until autumn before the fruit is bursting on the vine and ready for the *vendange* (grape harvest).

After the long cold winter, spring brings the château park to life.

12 APRIL

Our potager is a magical place. Partly surrounded by a stone wall, it's been neglected for many years. But nature finds a way.

Grapevines grow energetically along one wall. Our apple trees look a little sad, but most are still bearing fruit. We have cherry, peach and plum trees. A *noyer* (walnut tree) at one end has grown a little too large and threatens a wall of the Moulin Bigeard. We find rhubarb, *cassis* (blackcurrants), wild blackberries, quince and masses of Jerusalem artichokes.

In their heyday, the potager and orchard must have been enormous. We find traces of the original beds and six large water basins that still appear to be in good condition. We've cleared decades of rubbish out of the little *pavillon de potager* with its slate roof. Careful excavations have now revealed its original *tomette* floor.

Today we aggressively prune our grapevines to give them a chance of bearing fruit later in the season. We're eager to start planting but need to wait for a study with our architect. We want to respect its original design as much as possible.

The potager is home to one of France's best-preserved Éolienne Bollées. Like a contraption out of the world of Jules Verne, it's a wind turbine that towers almost fifteen metres over the potager garden. A spiral staircase winds around its cast-iron column. At the top of the fifty steps, a platform affords stupendous views of the surrounding countryside, although on windy days the swaying of the huge structure can be quite disconcerting.

It was constructed in 1900 by Édouard-Émile Lebert, who had acquired the famed Bollée manufacturing foundry in Le Mans in 1898. It was the job of Verrue's current mayor, Francis Siclet, to run the *éolienne* when he lived at the Moulin Bigeard in the early 1980s. This involved rising at 5 am to climb the *éolienne* in order to operate it.

His father looked after it decades before when he worked for the marquis. Francis tells us that his father descended deep underground to maintain the pump mechanism and the enormous reservoir, so large that you could drive a cart in it.

The Éolienne Bollée was installed to pump water from the huge underground reservoir below into a stone water tower (*château d'eau*) estimated to hold nine thousand litres and in turn to the *bassins* that watered the potager garden. At one time it would have also pumped water to the château itself.

Like the potager garden and the Moulin Bigeard, the wind turbine is *inscrit* as a *monument historique*. About three hundred and fifty were installed across France, of which around eighty are still standing.

We dream of one day restoring ours so that it can pump water into our potager again. One day!

Our potager is a magical place. Partly surrounded by a stone wall, it's been neglected for many years. But nature finds a way.

The Éolienne Bollée.

Today he has revealed the mystery of the identity of these two remarkable figures.

18 APRIL

Monsieur Anthony Bernard, a local amateur historian, has visited us at the château. For several years he has been preparing a booklet recounting the history of Purnon.

We're pleased to help – he has used various sources to gather information about the historical land purchases, family heraldry and genealogy to record some of the events that have occurred at Purnon.

When we purchased the château we acquired several unidentified portraits of what appear to be eighteenth-century personalities. On an earlier visit Monsieur Bernard inspected two of them closely – a man and a woman in matching gilded frames. He noted information on the back of the canvas as well as medals and awards that the sitters were wearing.

Today he has revealed the mystery of the identity of these two remarkable figures. Although not husband and wife as we had assumed, they both belong to the d'Oyron (or d'Oiron) family – two sisters of this family married Daniel de Rochequairie, who purchased Purnon in 1893.

The woman is Sophie Rose de Rosen-Kleinroop (1764–1828). She married the Prince de Broglie who fought alongside La Fayette during the American War of Independence. Both Sophie and her husband were imprisoned during the Terror at the height of the Revolution. The Prince was taken from the Conciergerie and guillotined. Incredibly Sophie escaped to Switzerland. She returned to France and married Marc-René de Voyer de Paulmy d'Argenson (1771–1842) a fervent supporter of Napoleon Bonaparte.

In 1827, one of their daughters married Pierre René Gustave Fournier de Boisayrault d'Oyron (1803–64). His father is the subject of the other portrait – Pierre Auguste Fournier de Boisayrault d'Oyron, Baron d'Oyron and Knight of the Royal Order of St Louis (1768–1837).

Pierre Auguste also led an eventful life. Taking part in the royalist invasion of Brittany during the fighting that followed the French Revolution, he was captured in Quiberon on 21 July 1795 along with twenty-eight others and sentenced to death eleven days later. As the executioners moved along the line of condemned men, the Baron d'Oyron emptied his pockets of gold coins. His guards were momentarily distracted by the prospect of loot and the Baron d'Oyron made his escape. After being hidden in a barn loft by a local woman for several days while search parties hunted for him, he lived another forty-one years and died peacefully in his bed on 23 January 1837 at the Château d'Oiron, a short drive from Purnon.

The d'Oyron family would be joined by marriage to the de Rochequairie family at the end of the nineteenth century, and one of the d'Oyron sisters must have brought these portraits of their great-grandparents to Purnon.

Piece by piece we are uncovering the history of Purnon and the remarkable stories of the families who have lived here.

Left: Sophie Rose de Rosen-Kleinroop (1764–1828).
Above: Pierre Auguste Fournier de Boisayrault d'Oyron (1768–1837).

19 APRIL

I've broken my thumb.

We've tried so hard to be safe – helmets, gloves, eye and hearing protection. We've been cautious on ladders.

As always, it happened when my guard was down.

I have been gradually removing kilometres of wire fences that crisscross the property. They were installed when the family grazed sheep in the paddocks to keep the grass low. Now, overgrown with grass, weeds and even trees, the fences are a hazard to both humans and wildlife. They are also an eyesore and an inconvenience. They will all have to come out.

The fences are supported by a mix of wooden and metal pickets. Some of the wire is single-strand, some barbed, most of it woven wire. In many places, new fencing was simply added over old wire whenever it collapsed. It's been suggested that I just use the tractor and rip it all out. But this will leave broken strands of wire and posts snapped at ground level everywhere. I want to collect all the wire and remove the posts properly so that in the future, tractors, mowers and machinery can pass safely across the fields.

While the tractor can help, most of it will have to be done by hand. It's tedious and demanding work.

But getting back to my thumb. Yesterday, while trying to loosen a wooden post that had been buried with rocks to add support, I jammed my thumb between the post and a rock.

When I woke this morning and surveyed the huge swelling, a trip to the Loudun hospital beckoned. An X-ray confirmed the break and now I'll be sporting a plaster cast on my dominant hand for six weeks.

22 APRIL

Flick has done an incredible job building our social media presence. She updates Instagram with a daily snapshot of what's happened at the château. So many people tell us that her posts are either the last thing they see before they go to bed or the first thing they look for when they wake up. For family and friends thousands of kilometres away in Australia, it's the only way they can connect with château life.

She's added wonderful content interviewing people connected with Purnon and translating for our English-speaking audience. The number of followers is growing rapidly.

A team from the television channel France 2 arrives at Purnon today. It's a great opportunity to spread the message about the rescue of Purnon to a wider audience.

3 MAY

Today we received our first order for Château de Purnon drink coasters.

An enormous quantity of beautiful slate has come off Purnon's roofs over the years. Intrigued, Flick set to work to consider a way to give this precious resource a second life. She ordered a tool to cut the slate and experimented with various felt pads. By carefully washing and then oiling the slate, she brings its aged patina to life.

Flick designed a presentation box – samples arrived and, after months of back and forth, she has finally settled on a tasteful weathered timber bearing a Purnon logo. We add a small reproduction of one of Purnon's historic postcards *et … voilà*. Elegant drink coasters.

It's an inspired idea – you can own a small part of the château's historic roof and your purchase will help finance its restoration.

It's not easy to ask others for financial support for our project, and we resolve that whatever we offer on the website boutique must be chic – no kitsch snow domes or tea towels here.

Clockwise from top left:
Slate tiles are transformed into elegant coasters
to help fund the roof restoration.
A terracotta vase – the last of eight that originally
sat atop Purnon's terraces.
The original *buanderie* (laundry) is home to three
ponnes (giant stone vats) used for heavy-duty washing.
Entering the small farmhouse.

*And suddenly Château de Purnon
has a family - Flick and Tim
and Mademoiselle Truffe*

9 MAY

Normally, the *lièvres* (hares) that we spot on our prairies are skittish and very quick to flee. So it comes as quite a shock when Flick finds a stubbornly stationary one seated on the grass next to a hedge on the *cour d'honneur*, right in front of the château. The explanation becomes quickly apparent. She has given birth to a litter of leverets. She has chosen a terrible place right next to our driveway, but obviously we can't move her. We put up some marker tape to keep curious onlookers away and prevent cars from using that part of the drive.

Over the next few days, the babies start to leave mum's care and take up residence in the nearby hedge. Eventually only one remains. But out in the open, they are easy prey for predators. A few days later, we sadly come across the carcass of one, still warm.

21 MAY

Every château needs a dog.

We had resolved to wait until we were settled and some major works concluded before we turned our minds to adding a hound, but serendipity has wagged its enthusiastic tail.

Nicole de Rochequairie's daughter Adrienne and her husband, Serge, own France's largest organic truffle farm not far from us near the town of Chinon. One of their truffle dogs, a Lagotto Romagnolo, had *une liaison nocturne* with an unknown neighbourhood dog and was now expecting puppies. Would we take one? The decision was made for us! After she gave birth to an adorable litter of seven puppies, the father, hitherto unknown, was revealed. A *berger australien* - an Australian Shepherd from a neighbouring winemaker! We arrived immediately to lay claim to the cutest puppy in the litter and instantly christened her Truffle. Serge and Adrienne's daughter, Victoria, was having none of it - the dog is French, so the name on her collar reads Truffe (rhymes with 'roof'). We now learn that *truffe* is also the French word for a dog's nose, because the snout so often resembles a black truffle. It seems the perfect name.

After eight weeks she had been weaned with her littermates and we arrive to collect her. She's apprehensive on the drive home. It must be a terrifying shock to spend her first night away from her mum and her siblings. We shamelessly shower her with affection and let her sleep on the end of our bed - any authority is lost.

And suddenly Château de Purnon has a family - Flick and Tim and Mademoiselle Truffe. She has made herself right at home, as though every dog should live in a house with a hundred and five rooms large and small to explore.

If we can repair the ceiling and the roof above it, we are optimistic that once again the stables can be home to horses.

29 MAY

Finally, my new ride-on mower has arrived. It has a wide cutting blade, zero turn (perfect for manoeuvring around the château's stone terrace walls) and it mulches while it cuts. It's a big investment but an enormous time saver. Suddenly, maintaining the château's lawns becomes a joy instead of the bone-crushing frustration that had accompanied the use of the now departed International tractor. But within a couple of days I've managed to puncture both the main tyres. Suitably chastened, I present myself at our local garage. Anthony supplies an anti-puncture treatment that does the trick.

Over the coming months, José and I compete for the fastest time to cut the grass on the *cour d'honneur*. Despite my wider cutting blade, José has a more experienced eye. His greater efficiency secures the fastest time – a very respectable seventeen minutes.

7 JUNE

José and I spend the morning putting up almost fifty Saugnac gauges that will allow us to measure gradual movement in a number of Purnon's buildings.

The *communs ouest* (western outbuilding), housing our chapel, stables and tack rooms, is particularly problematic. It has shifted enormously. At its northern end, a massive modern structural support has been attached to the rear of the building. If you look along the front of the *communs*, a disconcerting bend is clearly apparent. Sadly, our tack rooms cannot be saved. The floors have buckled, and sections of the internal stone walls have collapsed as the back of the building began to sink. Remarkably, the beautiful wood panelling has moved with the building and is still in perfect condition! Walking though the various rooms is quite discombobulating, as though you've had several glasses of cognac too many.

The stables are another matter. They house four loose horse boxes and eight stalls. Many superb features remain: a grand stone entrance, a brass bell, even the original drinking troughs. If we can repair the ceiling and the roof above it, we are optimistic that once again the stables can be home to horses.

But the gauges will provide the vital evidence as to whether the huge structural support has worked and the building has stopped shifting. We place others on the *orangerie*, the Moulin Bigeard and the *communs est*.

8 JUNE

Today we welcome Éliane Autin to the château. Éliane lived in the *ancien logement*, the home attached to the end of the *communs est*. 'I was born here,' she declares, entering one particular room. Tears well as she recognises the now peeling wallpapers from her childhood and recalls the first time her family had hot water. Their only toilet was a shared outdoor latrine by the nearby *basse-cour* wall. Her mother was a cook in the château kitchen and her father, after returning from the war as a prisoner of the Germans, worked as a farmhand. Éliane spots the etched name Napi on a stone wall, an Italian family who stayed at Purnon, refugees during the war. And then she spots her own name, engraved perhaps seventy years ago! She is ashamed but we are secretly thrilled. This rebellious act as a child has immortalised her in the history of Purnon.

We gaze up at the roof above where the loft used to be.

15 JUNE

In politics we used to joke that the ship of state is the only ship that leaks from the top.

Purnon is a hardly a ship, but the leaking château roof is the cause of much stress. Our system of buckets and plastic sheeting needs constant attention.

When heavy rains come, the water passes through the *grenier* and collects on the second floor, where the water damage is significant. In severe downpours it runs down the main staircase. It's a depressing sight. We are desperate for the main works on our roof to commence and give us some respite.

Today, José, Flick and I spent a few hours trying to improve our system for tackling the leaks in the *grenier*. The smallest adjustment in just the right place can redirect enormous volumes of water. José was fixing some gaps when, to our horror, the flooring gave way and he found himself dangling through to the second floor. We urged him to use the stairs next time. Despite our banter, we all got quite a shock.

1 JULY

We've decided to start work on the interior of *la petite maison de la ferme*, the small farmhouse behind the *communs ouest* and next to our old *chai*.

The first task is to lift the *tomette* tiles. They come up pretty easily with the aid of a wrecking bar. Many broken ones are discarded and we put the rest aside to be cleaned later.

Next we take down the plasterboard ceiling in the central room. It's low, and we'd like to expose the roof above to give the room a sense of volume and space. The plaster comes down quickly but the wooden floor in the attic above proves more stubborn. Eventually it yields and we gaze up at the roof above where the loft used to be. A very satisfying morning's work.

Abandoned for decades, it will be some time before the small farmhouse can be brought back to life.

THE LEAKING CHÂTEAU ROOF IS THE CAUSE OF MUCH STRESS.

Sunlight piercing the château roof betrays
its fragile condition.

3 JULY

Lunch with Madame Dominique Henriot, a wonderful lady who contacted us shortly after our arrival. Her connection with Purnon is strong, as the château's hunting dogs used to be housed in large kennels that once occupied part of her estate. She has a soft spot for Australians and we instantly warm to her.

She lives only a few minutes away, at the other end of the Forêt de Scévolles from Purnon. Her remarkable property, concealed in the forest, was built as a hunting lodge at the beginning of the nineteenth century in a style known as Directoire. It exhibits a similar obsession with symmetry to Purnon but, in keeping with the political tastes of post-revolutionary France, in a slightly more restrained tone. It has been immaculately restored. Her French gardens are amazing. In the dining room on the ground floor I find wallpaper hand-painted by Carle Vernet depicting 'La Chasse à Compiègne'. Completely restored, it is a masterpiece of national importance.

She is a wonderful host, well informed about her guests, and each stage of the lunch lasts the perfect duration. It's a masterclass in French private hospitality. We speak in French for the entire lunch, a considerable accomplishment for Flick and me.

14 JULY

La fête nationale (no French person calls it Bastille Day) - the fourteenth of July. The village rocks to fireworks, music and dancing. A march to the *monument aux morts*, a rendition of la Marseillaise and a short speech from Mayor Francis Siclet remind us that this is a country that suffered terribly at the hands of the wars of the twentieth century.

The afternoon features an egg-and-spoon race (yes!) and a tug of war that quickly descends into a competition between Purnon and Verrue. Thankfully, some of the stronger folks in the village are allocated to the château team. And the mayor intervenes outrageously to ensure that when teams of children battle it out, no one ever seems to get the upper hand.

As the sun sets, the children of the village are led through the streets on a lantern parade.

Mayor Francis quietly thanks Flick, Truffe and me for attending. It's been a long time since anyone from the château joined the celebrations. We drop in on Nicole as we walk home. I get the impression that celebrating the storming of the Bastille and the French Revolution is a divisive topic amongst some French people.

Clockwise from top left:
Scattered throughout the château lie more than two centuries of fabrics, garments and millinery.
The impeccable Madame Dominique Henriot.
Flick joins the celebrations of *la fête nationale*.

THE WALL IS GRADUALLY DRAGGING DOWN THE SIDE OF THE BARREL ROOM, AND IF WE DON'T ACT SOON WE'LL LOSE OUR CHARMING CHAI.

17 JULY

It's a nervous day at the château.

In French they say *'on ne fait pas d'omelette sans casser des oeufs'* - you can't make an omelette without breaking some eggs. Alain Costa and his team will attempt to take down a stone wall of a barn attached to our *chai*. The wall is gradually dragging down the side of the barrel room, and if we don't act soon we'll lose our charming *chai*. Monsieur Didier has approved the project, but I can see Alain Costa hesitating. It's not an easy project to execute safely. Done poorly, we could break plenty of eggs with no omelette to show for it.

We cut down the last trees that block our access. The telescopic tractor arrives and a metal brace attached to the wall is cut. A few strategic blows with the heavy machinery and the wall tumbles. The *chai* is untouched! It's a triumph, and we all breathe a sigh of relief. Afterwards, Alain confesses that he had a sleepless night worrying about the project.

Purnon's *chai* - a relic of the estate's winemaking past.

19 JULY

To succeed, first you have to take the plunge.

As we leap into Purnon's restored pool this afternoon, we certainly feel we've held nothing back.

Adding a pool to a heritage-listed château can be high risk. Poorly executed, pools can be an absolute visual blight. Purnon's pool, a tastefully constructed 1990s addition, was in a terrible state by the time we acquired the château. The liner was gone, a tree was emerging through its cracked concrete floor and weeds had overgrown the blackened terrace that surrounded it.

We decided to dispense with the deep end: in the long term, it will be cheaper to treat and circulate the reduced volume of water. Twenty-seven tonnes of broken bricks and tiles collected from around the estate have to be dumped into the pool to level it.

Flick sets to work clearing the pool precinct of a decade's worth of weeds and sows wildflower seeds in their place. A lawn is planted and hundreds of dahlia bulbs from around the château are relocated. We clean out the buildings beside the pool and carry out some minor roof repairs. A new concrete base is laid and a new liner installed. Later a new pump and filtration system are connected. The only thing left is to fill it with water.

We had resolved to have it ready for summer. Our pool technician is infuriatingly slow, but so far summer has been wet and cold. But on the first day that the mercury nudges above thirty degrees, we can finally take the plunge!

It's an omen.

28 JULY

José's sister, Solange, has finished renovating her new holiday home opposite the Moulin Bigeard. She is our closest neighbour, and her home has a great history. It served as a pharmacy for the poor, a hospital during the Franco-Prussian War of 1870-71 and a school run by nuns until 1904. More recently it was the home of General Roger de Ruffray, a celebrated French officer who piloted the last plane to take off from the besieged French base at Dien Bien Phu during the war in Indochina.

Solange's son Corentin is staying with a group of his former scouting friends. She makes their stay conditional upon them working for a day at Purnon.

Eleven fit young people arrive - with José, Richard (an old schoolfriend of mine who is visiting from Saudi Arabia), Flick and me, we get a lot done. It's marvellous to see tasks that would have consumed days finished in a few hours. Afterwards we have drinks and a tour of the château. We're always struck by how interested and knowledgeable young people in Europe are regarding their built heritage.

Our suave real estate agent Guillaume looks on as I inspect the pool on our first visit to Purnon. In a year and a half we'll swim in it for the first time.

*By evening, the sun is still high in the sky.
Most nights we eat dinner on the bridge
at the back of the château. These are some
of the happiest times.*

10 AUGUST

At Purnon, the summer days seem to extend forever. The morning sun wakes me well before my alarm, and for a moment I panic and think that I must have overslept as it seems to have been light forever. Some days are impossibly hot and, combined with the sheer physicality of the work in the park, I just can't drink enough to stay hydrated. By mid-afternoon I am completely and utterly exhausted. With hours and hours of daylight left, it is impossible to keep going, and yet, with so much to do, we refuse to stop and waste the precious daylight.

By evening, the sun is still high in the sky. Most nights we eat dinner on the bridge at the back of the château. These are some of the happiest times. Often *chevreuils* graze in the park, our own private safari. With still hours of sunlight remaining, the temperature warm but not stifling and our bodies aching after the day's exertions, finally we can relax and enjoy the peace around us, guilt-free.

18 AUGUST

We've snuck away from Purnon to participate in a day of visits to heritage-listed properties in our department of Vienne. It's been organised by the VMF (Vieilles Maisons Françaises), one of the two main membership-based heritage organisations in France. It's fascinating to be invited into listed private properties that have been restored with great care and to chat with the owners about their journey to preserve their homes. We join a large and welcoming group and drive to each property in succession. Over lunch, the VMF formally introduces us to the assembled crowd, and one of our good friends, Bertrand de Feydeau, explains the project at Purnon to the group. There is considerable enthusiasm, and many of the people who approach us afterwards to chat are surprisingly well-informed about Purnon.

It's a very worthwhile day, not only because we are able to see heritage works set in private homes but also because raising the profile of Purnon improves our chances of securing philanthropic support in the form of prizes that are awarded by these associations.

21 AUGUST

Flick has bought me an impressive brass-mounted telescope for my birthday and, as the sun rises, we spot an enormous *cerf* haughtily poised like a colossus on the *grand allée*, his massive antlers visible even to the naked eye.

25 AUGUST

When Bill Bryson wrote his travelogue about Australia, he marvelled at the range of fatal hazards that awaited the unsuspecting visitor. Australia's reputation as a land of deadly creatures is raised regularly with us - crocs, sharks, spiders, even box jellyfish.

Having survived Australia's perils, it therefore comes as quite a shock that it is in rural France that Flick has been bitten by an asp viper. Clearing a section of the woods with Eve, Flick was bitten through her glove on her left hand. The fang marks are clearly visible. The paralysed hand requires another trip to the Loudun hospital. The ache of the bite lingers for months.

5 SEPTEMBER

As we clear the château room by room we come across coins - under carpets, behind furniture, at the back of drawers. Many of them are from recent times, the decades before France adopted the euro in 1999.

But occasionally we come across a real gem. I've amassed a set from the Vichy regime, when a puppet French government ruled France under German occupation during the Second World War. They're not especially rare or valuable, but bearing their patriotic slogan of *Travail*, *famille*, *patrie* (work, family, homeland), which replaced *Liberté*, *égalité*, *fraternité*, it's a reminder of the Orwellian doublespeak of those dark totalitarian times.

We find a respectable set from the Second Empire, with the distinctive visage of Napoleon III clearly recognisable. And then a real treasure: a coin from the kingdom of Italy dated 1810, with the face of a young Napoleon Bonaparte in profile.

Today I've stumbled on our most bizarre discovery so far. While working in the *basse-cour*, my eye spots a small round object lying in the dirt. Perhaps it's one of Purnon's hunting buttons, which adorned the jackets of the château's hunters. I've been eager to gather some.

On closer inspection the bronze disc reveals itself to be a coin, one side showing two heads in profile facing away and the unmistakeable letters 'IMP'. The other side is marked by what looks like a crocodile. Some online research confirms our hunch. It's a Roman coin from the era of Augustus, the first Roman emperor. The crocodile represents the Roman city of Nîmes in France, and the two faces are Augustus and his lieutenant Agrippa. The coin is over two thousand years old!

But how did it come to rest in Purnon's *basse-cour*? Has it really lain there since just after Caesar's conquest of Gaul? Or was it part of someone's nineteenth-century coin-collecting passion, picked up on a grand tour through Italy?

Today I've stumbled on our most bizarre discovery so far.

Clockwise from top left:
Crafted by the château's carpenters, one of Purnon's original beds.
Augustus and Agrippa - but how did they come to rest in Purnon's *basse-cour*?
The window above the *grand escalier* captures the fading sun - a small piece of the genius of Purnon's design.
The reverse side of the coin with the Roman name for the city Nîmes and its symbol, the crocodile, discernible.

9 SEPTEMBER

We're planning to showcase the *four à pain* in Purnon's *boulangerie* for this year's *journées du patrimoine*. At the back of the *boulangerie* sits a small room filled with junk. José and I set to work clearing it out and it reveals an old *pétrin*, a giant wooden kneading table. We spot a *tomette* tile beneath layers of packed earth. Soon we're digging enthusiastically, and fifteen wheelbarrow-loads of soil later we're admiring the original *tomette* floor. It's a *boulangerie* fit for a king - or a marquis, at least!

That evening, José and his sister, Solange, introduce us to the *brame du cerf*.

It's the rutting season for the *cerfs* in the Forêt de Scévolles. From late August through to October, the forest echoes with the impressive, almost prehistoric cries (*brame*) of the *cerfs* as they mark their territory and endeavour to warn off rivals.

After the sun sets, we make our way to secret spots within the forest where we can admire the sound. We wait silently and the cries echo around us. They appear to be very close.

11 SEPTEMBER

It's all systems go as we prepare for Château de Purnon's second open day for the *journées du patrimoine*. This year we won't have the same level of support from the councillors and staff at the commune - it seems some locals grumbled about municipal resources helping out at the château. We have been welcomed so warmly that I must admit to being a little disheartened to learn that some people feel that way.

But experience tells us what needs to be done to prepare the property. Today we've organised a working bee (a phrase that, we've learned, doesn't translate well beyond Australian English). A dozen volunteers set to work clearing our dry moat, and once again we watch work that would have taken us all week disappearing over the course of an afternoon.

There's a great team spirit, and several of the volunteers offer to return the following week to help us when the crowds arrive.

18–19 SEPTEMBER

The *journées du patrimoine* has proven a giant success. This year we opened over two days. Saturday was wet and slow, perhaps around three hundred people. But on Sunday, the weather blessed us and around seven hundred people came to take a look.

We teamed up with Emmanuelle and her husband, Benoît, who run the Maison Martin *boulangerie* in nearby Mirebeau. They expertly use Purnon's magnificent eighteenth-century *four à pain*, restored last year by Alain Costa. Benoît has heated it slowly over the previous three days. He uses an infrared laser thermometer to show me the surprising variation in the temperature across various parts of the brick oven.

Meanwhile, we have formed a wonderful friendship with Kate, Benjamin and their daughter Izzy at Domaine Ampelidae. Their organic wines are amongst the best in the Haut Poitou wine region. They've helped us create a *bar à vin* (wine bar) next to the *boulangerie* in front of the *communs est*.

What could possibly be more French than admiring the view of Château de Purnon with a glass of cabernet franc perched on an atmospheric Bordeaux oak wine barrel while the aroma of baking bread wafts gently across the *cour d'honneur*? *La vie est belle!*

The Comtesse Nicole de Rochequairie arrives. She alights from the car like royalty, and the crowd is hushed as she is swept towards the *boulangerie*. A congregation of eager onlookers hangs on every word while she holds court, planting herself on the terrace as her subjects wait politely for an audience. For a republic, France still loves its nobles.

Our team of volunteers work fabulously over the two days. Eve and her boyfriend, Guillaume, create a fierce rivalry to see who can make the most sales in the *boulangerie* and the château shop where our *ardoise* tile coasters and Purnon prints are offered.

Frédéric - a volunteer from the previous weekend - offers brochures at the main gate explaining the various activities. Nanette, an Australian volunteer currently travelling around Europe, helps with the various picnic hamper orders, while I don a high-vis vest and direct traffic in the car park.

Flick greets senators, local mayors and friends old and new who descend on Purnon to show their support for our project and see the work so far.

By Sunday evening we are all exhausted but elated that so many people came to admire the château. There is a wonderful feeling of goodwill and anticipation that the major works will be commencing very soon.

The *pétrin* table originally used for kneading dough.

1 OCTOBER

A major step in Purnon's rebirth as we sign all of the contracts for the stage one works.

This will be the biggest tranche of the redevelopment. It's expected to take two years and it will be the largest investment in safeguarding the château since its construction almost two hundred and fifty years ago. It is the most urgent stage that will literally save Purnon from impending ruin.

The various contracts are divided by trade:
- *Maçonnerie*: all of the stonework on the château's façades and ten chimneys, as well as the bridge that traverses the dry moat at the back of the château.
- *Charpente*: the restoration of the immense wooden frame that supports the roof.
- *Couverture*: the replacement and installation of the 47,000 *ardoise* roof tiles.
- *Menuiserie*: two joinery projects to restore or replace all of the woodwork on Purnon's window shutters (as well as the window frames themselves on the second floor and in the attic).
- *Peinture*: the painting of all the restored joinery.
- *Restauration de sculpture*: the restoration of the royal busts and the return of these statues to the roof of Purnon, as well as works to restore and protect other statues on the château façades.

Keeping the budget under control is proving challenging. Some increases have been unavoidable – a rise in the cost of global copper, for example, means that the price of the 94,000 copper nails that will hold the *ardoise* tiles in place has also risen.

After some intense negotiations, Monsieur Didier has assembled the selected companies on site for a final briefing before the works can commence. We gather around the huge dining room table in the *salle à manger*.

The stage one works will proceed in two phases. First, the château's eastern side will be encased in scaffolding and all the trades will work off this platform to complete that side of the building. Then the massive scaffolding structure will be relocated to the western side.

Monsieur Didier addresses the men (yes, they are all men) in lofty and inspiring terms. Flick and I are surprised and humbled by how proud they seem to be to work on this project. They show us examples of other projects they have worked on. We are touched by the obvious skill, experience and enthusiasm they bring to their work.

Flick signs the fourteen contracts on behalf of both of us – our life savings are on the line. We are desperate for the works to begin as our system of buckets and plastic sheeting is struggling to protect the deteriorating roof. We've crossed the Rubicon.

A major step in Purnon's rebirth as we sign all of the contracts for the stage one works.

We are desperate for the works to begin as our system of buckets and plastic sheeting is struggling to protect the deteriorating roof. We've crossed the Rubicon.

Monsieur Didier guides us through contracts for the restoration of the château.

2 OCTOBER

Yesterday we received a call from our friend Fiona Beeston, a highly regarded winemaker from the town of Chinon. Her wines grace the lists of renowned Paris establishments such as Le George V, Le Taillevent and L'Arpège.

Fiona informs us that the time to harvest her grapes has arrived. It's a narrow window dependent on the current ripeness of the grapes and her estimate of the weather conditions over the next twenty-four hours.

We are thrilled to be invited to participate in the *vendange* (grape harvest), a French tradition. We arrive early on Saturday morning at Fiona's enchanting estate. The one and a half hectares of vines cling to the side of a hill close to the centre of town, the rising mist gradually revealing the medieval royal fortress that towers over Chinon. Croissants and coffee provide the fuel and we are all handed small secateurs and a bucket. Handpicked grapes are harvested according to a strict tradition. We work in groups of two, moving along opposite sides of the vines. When the bucket is full, you call out, '*Hotteur*' and a *porteur* appears carrying a large grape hod on their back, who in turn tips the grapes into crates. We work fast as rain is forecast for the afternoon, but it's great fun. We stop for morning tea, but there is no tea in sight – clearly it's never too early to enjoy a glass of wine in France.

By noon we are finished. The cabernet franc we've just picked is already being destemmed and crushed in the *chai*. Some of the grape juice is offered to sample. We wander into Fiona's charming home where an enormous table extends the entire length of the entrance – it must seat more than forty people. Earlier vintages of her Clos des Capucins dating back to 2011 are offered. William Bernet, owner and chef of Le Severo, a renowned Parisian restaurant, arrives and prepares a barbecue. It's a sublime experience to drink superb wines, made from grapes grown only a few metres from where we are sitting, and eating food prepared by a Parisian chef while admiring the view over the historic fortress of Chinon and the surrounding town. Gently, the rain starts to fall.

3 OCTOBER

We are again Dominique Henriot's guests, but this time we are on a mission. She has organised for us to dine with one of her great friends, Monsieur Benoît Bassi, who is president of the Fondation Mérimée, a philanthropic organisation dedicated to preserving French heritage.

Dominique phones us the evening before to check that we are '*en forme*' (roughly, 'fighting fit'). She emphasises the importance of making a strong impression on him. Monsieur Didier joins us and we pitch our project to Monsieur Bassi enthusiastically. After lunch we adjourn to Purnon and spend several hours introducing him to the château.

Meetings like this are vital to mobilise the immense financial resources that restoring Purnon is starting to consume. Our original estimates of the cost of the restoration are proving hopelessly optimistic. We always understood that the money would run out at some point. But the complexity of the works and the extent of the deterioration is far greater than we imagined.

The *vendange* at Clos des Capucins.

4 OCTOBER

With les *journées du patrimoine* behind us for another year, we can return our attention to uncovering Purnon's network of stone gutters. The task has become something of an obsession.

Flick and I have set to work on the system that must lie covered in front of the *communs ouest*. We commence at the door of the chapel. It becomes apparent that the gutters here are enormous, extending two metres in front of the building. As we work outwards from the door, a path starts to appear. We are amazed as the grass and soil give way to these stones that have laid buried twenty centimetres below. As we uncover the path that rises towards the hedges, we can begin to discern more clearly the ingenious design that lay behind it.

As always, José arrives to lend a hand. His practical and logical brain is in overdrive as he tries to understand what we are uncovering. I can see him inspecting several concrete covers that lie along the retaining wall near the path we are unearthing. We strike a concrete pipe that lies beneath the soil but above the original stone gutters. It must have been laid in the twentieth century when the layer of earth was put down. I grab a crowbar and with some effort we prise open the first of the covers. It's water to a depth of about a metre with an overflow outlet that links to whatever lies beneath the second cover. With a bit more pressure, we lift this cover and find what appears to be a gravel filtration system. It drains from the bottom. But to where?

Both of us eye off the third and final cover. It's larger, heavier and almost impossible to lift. But finally it gives way. A vaulted cavern descends into the darkness below – the echo of our astonished voices testifies to its enormous proportions. José immediately notices the *tuffeau* stone walls. The cover may be concrete and therefore somewhat modern, but this reservoir must date back to the original construction of the château. We can hear water slowly dripping in from an inlet connected to the two neighbouring filters. We attach a weight to a length of rope and measure the depth – it's over five metres!

Our sense of adventure takes over and I fetch a ladder narrow enough to lower through the entrance of the cistern. It's not long enough to reach the bottom and so we secure it stoutly with ropes to the back of the car. I don a head torch and José attaches a separate belay rope firmly around me in case of catastrophe. I tentatively descend the ladder. In the half-light of the torch I can see that the cistern is large, curved about five metres wide. The water level is high so I can only descend so far, but I can see an inlet in the ceiling through which the water collected from the roof of the *communs ouest* arrives in the cistern via the gravel filtration system.

But what was the water used for? A nineteenth-century hand pump is attached to a wall above the cistern.

With the various wells and cisterns we have already uncovered around the estate as well as the extensive network of stone tunnels and gutters that channelled rain collected on the vast château and *communs* roofs, I'm beginning to realise that water collection and diversion lay at the heart of Purnon's clever design.

The château's enormous roof, along with those of the two *communs*, would have collected vast quantities of water when it rained. Diverting and then collecting that water was vital not only for human consumption and the gardens, but also to protect the stability of these huge stone buildings.

The morning sun awakens the chapel.

Ciels de lit (bed canopies) and curtain pelmets
rescued from the attic.

9 OCTOBER

Another successful volunteer day at the château. During Monsieur Didier's last visit we showed him further stone gutters that José and I had uncovered on the château's east and south-east side in the moat. He was impressed both by the excellent condition of the stone and also the volume of earth we had moved. I explained that despite several *sondages* (tests), we had been unable to find traces of more gutters on the south-west or western sides. Monsieur Didier insists they will be there and urges us to try again.

So we dedicate the day to finding and uncovering these stone gutters. Finally we locate them lying thirty or forty centimetres beneath the surface, some of the deepest we've encountered. But Monsieur Didier is spot on. Thirteen trailer-loads of earth later and they lie before us, complete with stone steps up to the external basement door. We've moved so much earth – previously this door appeared to be at ground level!

The elevated humidity levels in the *cave à vin* on that side of the château have previously troubled me. Perhaps the presence of tonnes of earth packed against the side and back of the basement walls provides part of the explanation.

> *The elevated humidity levels in the* cave à vin *on that side of the château have previously troubled me. Perhaps the presence of tonnes of earth packed against the side and back of the basement walls provides part of the explanation.*

Have we found the cause of the humidity levels in the basement?

16 OCTOBER

We awake to a wonderful feature on our project gracing the front cover of the *Good Weekend* magazine back in Australia. It's a great escapist story that seems to have struck a chord as we receive hundreds of messages from friends and family in Australia, plus others we had lost contact with over the decades and other people inspired by the project. Our Instagram followers start to climb - by the end of the weekend we have added eight thousand. People buy our slate coasters and make donations. It's wonderful for our morale.

Later in the morning, Monsieur Didier arrives for an onsite meeting with two of the companies. He's here to inspect the stone samples that stonemasons Soporen have selected. They need to match the aged tones of the existing château *tuffeau* in both yellow and white. It's not just a matter of selecting the right quarry - all of the stone needs to be extracted from the same section of the quarry so the hue is consistent.

The team from FP Couverture arrives with the *ardoise* roof tile samples. Sourced from Galicia in Spain, some are machine cut while others are cut by hand. Under sunlight, the difference is surprising.

We review the plans for the scaffolding and the site access, parking and materials storage arrangements to ensure that Purnon's fragile terraces will all be protected. We are impatient to start.

Mademoiselle Truffe holds court in the *grand salon*.

25 OCTOBER

We have a rat plague. I have to confess to being traumatised by the signs of these awful rodents. They devour everything. They chew through plaster walls and wooden doors and gnaw at electrical cabling. Our kitchen compost container and Truffe's food are attacked. We repair the plaster along their preferred routes and lace it with shards of broken glass, hoping to mortally injure these haemophiliac vermin.

We've disposed of four so far but the mousetraps we bought online are proving pathetically small. We're reluctant to use rat poison. Truffe eats everything she encounters, and the thought of her chewing on a rodent carcass laced with poison in some hidden corner of the château is too distressing to contemplate.

We resort to more medieval methods. When we hear their telltale scurrying, I give chase with a large plastic container. With a rat trapped inside, we at first tried to administer the poison. But they're too clever. I'm forced to bludgeon them with a saucepan instead. One of them escapes and I run him through with a fencing rapier that happens to be lying conveniently nearby. It seems a more noble end than being crushed by a frying pan.

La vie (et mort) au château!

28 OCTOBER

The team from Artisan du Bois arrives to commence the removal of the château's *volets* (window shutters). Many must come down before the assembly of the scaffolding or they will be trapped against the building. Most are original and some are in surprisingly good condition despite their age. They can be restored and returned. Others are severely degraded or missing altogether and will have to be replaced. A huge cherry picker helps with the task and each shutter is carefully indexed so it can be returned to its proper place after restoration.

Purnon's original window shutters. Some have been lost, most will be restored.

PURNON'S TREASURES INCLUDE A UNIQUE COLLECTION OF ORIGINAL EIGHTEENTH-CENTURY WALLPAPERS.

Left: The ground-floor dressing room with its handcrafted wallpaper panels.
Right: A well-preserved wallpaper from the 1830s that graces a first-floor dressing room.

30 OCTOBER

Purnon's treasures include a unique collection of original eighteenth-century wallpapers.

We fell in love with the beautiful, rich hand-painted blue arabesques with nesting bird motifs in a first-floor bedroom on our initial visit. The wallpapers gracing all four walls are in surprisingly good condition. We somewhat unimaginatively christened this room the blue room until Nicole de Rochequairie told us it was the room she slept in on her first night at the château in the late 1960s. Now it is Nicole's room.

On the ground floor on the western side of the château, a small dressing room is graced by an exquisite paper with allegories of peace and puttos (think chubby naked male children).

I've contacted the Musée du Papier Peint in Rixheim in eastern France to see if I can learn more about these and other wallpapers at Purnon. They respond with great excitement. The blue wallpaper is from the Manufacture Réveillon, the most celebrated of France's eighteenth-century wallpaper workshops. Although they have a record of this design in an album from the Réveillon workshop, there is no known surviving example of it other than at Purnon! We have four complete walls in remarkable condition.

The Réveillon workshop in the working-class Paris neighbourhood of Faubourg Saint-Antoine was the scene of some of the worst violence of the French Revolution. The owner, Jean-Baptiste Réveillon, an unusually progressive employer, commented on wages and bread prices. His words were twisted out of context and an angry mob destroyed his workshop and home. He and his family fled to the safety of the Bastille just in time. A confrontation between soldiers and the riotous horde ensured. Shots were fired, first into the air and then into the crowd. Hundreds were killed and injured. Several instigators and looters were caught and hanged and others sentenced to brutal terms of forced labour on naval galleys. The Réveillon riots over several days would prove to be the bloodiest of the Revolution.

It's a sobering thought that our wallpaper would have been made by many of the same people who bore witness to these tumultuous events.

The wallpaper from the small dressing room on the ground floor is also extremely rare. The workshop and artist are unknown but just three examples still exist today, and those at Purnon appear to be the only panels that remain in situ.

The motifs include Mercury (the Roman god of commerce) and the design appears to celebrate the Eden Agreement, a commercial treaty between France and Great Britain signed in 1786. Infused with the free trade spirit of the time, the treaty was quickly seen as disadvantageous to France. Its adverse economic consequences fuelled the many grievances that would lead to revolution.

A third wallpaper in a first-floor dressing room is from the 1830s. While not dating from Purnon's construction, its age and repeating floral pattern with well-preserved colours make it a design worthy of careful preservation.

However, it has become apparent that the water damage and general dampness throughout parts of the château is starting to threaten the extraordinary blue wallpaper panels in Nicole's room. We ring Monsieur Didier and discuss taking one panel down as a matter of urgency. He is hesitant. If we leave it, forecast rain and storms could damage it beyond repair. But if we are clumsy, taking it down could also pose significant risks. We send him photos. He immediately consents to its removal, and we spend a nervous morning carefully prising the wooden frames away so that the wallpaper panel mounted on its original hessian *toile de jute* backing can be preserved.

31 OCTOBER

'The communes [villages] of France have a special love for those men and women whose lives have traversed an entire century.'

Mayor Francis Siclet has donned his mayoral robes and the entire village of Verrue has assembled in the village hall to pay homage to his mother, Madame Fernande Siclet, born in Verrue on 31 October 1921 and turning one hundred today. Married at age sixteen, mother of twelve children, grandmother to twenty-seven grandchildren, great-grandmother to thirty-eight great-grandchildren and great-great-grandmother to seven (so far) great-great-grandchildren. She is presented with a special coin struck by the commune. It's a touching moment. Her enormous family across many generations share the cramped space with friends and well-wishers from the village. A life spanning a century in which she has remained in this same tiny village is a reminder of an era that is fading before us.

And here we are: Madame Siclet - the oldest resident in Verrue - and Flick and I, the village's newest arrivals. We are surrounded by so many new friends that our incredible adventure over the last year and a half has blessed us with. Next week the scaffolding will be assembled, finally marking the official commencement of the stage one works on our journey to save Château de Purnon.

The exquisite Réveillon wallpaper.

Left: An incredible discovery. An original wallpaper
that survived the decay on the second floor.
Right: Fragments of an eighteenth-century wallpaper
uncovered during a bathroom restoration.

Raising
THE ROOF

VOULOIR, C'EST POUVOIR.

To want is to be able to.
(Where there's a will there's a way.)

2 NOVEMBER

After more than a year of study and preparation, our stage one works finally commence.

The Soporen team arrive and begin the immense task of putting up the scaffolding. It will take weeks before the entire eastern half of the château is encased in the huge metal frame.

And then welcome news arrives with *la poste*: the French Heritage Society has awarded Purnon a grant to support the stage one works on her roof and façades. The FHS is an American not-for-profit that funds projects in France and the US to safeguard and preserve French architectural heritage.

With the epic cost of the works now fully apparent, this financial support could not have come at a better time. We are incredibly grateful that enthusiasts in the US who share our passion for preserving remarkable places like Château de Purnon are willing to help us on our journey. It's also wonderful for our morale. With each prize and grant and donation, we are acutely aware that more and more of Purnon will be able to be restored on our watch.

3 NOVEMBER

Flick and I are guests at Château de la Mothe Chandeniers about thirty minutes north of Purnon.

Destroyed by fire in 1932, the château lay abandoned for decades. Trees gradually moved into the ruined turrets and its moat was slowly overtaken by nature and time. And then, in 2017, an extraordinary global crowd-funding campaign sold fifty-euro shares in a project of restoration that has raised millions of euros. The restoration will seek to preserve the wild romance of one of France's most photogenic buildings.

One of Purnon's volunteers, Stefan, organises volunteer days here at La Mothe Chandeniers and has arranged a private tour with the château's caretakers. For once we visit a château with restoration problems far more complex than we will ever face!

Unlike Purnon, there is no intention to attempt a complete restoration. The château itself will be stabilised and metal platforms will enable viewers to access different levels. Many remarkable original features have been preserved or rediscovered. It gives us hope to see a building destroyed and abandoned receiving a new life. The team exudes energy and innovation. It's a spirit we are determined to emulate.

Hand-blown eighteenth-century glass awaits the restoration of the frame and shutters that have protected it for more than two centuries.

Purnon under scaffolding, which will eventually
reach above the chimneys.

10 NOVEMBER

Alain Costa's team is working on repairing the stonework on the corner of the *chai* where the *hangar* (barn) wall was demolished. First they lay a concrete base, then they craft replacement *tuffeau* stone blocks a few at a time, allow each to set and dry in place with limestone mortar and then return a few days later to continue.

11 NOVEMBER

Armistice Day in the village of Verrue. A small crowd gathers at the *monument aux morts* with several veterans from conflicts in Algeria and Tunisia. A wreath is laid and Mayor Siclet gives a short address. We retire to the *salle des fêtes* for un *petit verre*.

The carnage of the First World War exacerbated a demographic crisis in France. Many small villages have never recovered. Verrue had a population of over a thousand people in the 1890s - today there are less than four hundred. An ageing population, the drift to the cities, war and changing economic conditions have all played a part. Perhaps our project at Purnon is a small step to help keep life and spirit in this tiny community.

15 NOVEMBER

A week's work commences clearing the vegetation that has overgrown the woods on the western side of the château. Completely hidden in this section is a small ruined stone building. We've been told it was the gardener's storehouse. Crushed by falling trees, there is not much left today, but we can make out the original entrance with the wooden door still in place. Fragments of its clay tiled roof lay scattered around the ruins, and several large beams haphazardly crisscross remnants of the walls and windows. This is one structure that we can never restore!

Flick ponders the work required to restore our *chai's* collapsed roof.

The oldest fixed object on the property is, surprisingly, the bell that sits above the chapel.

20 NOVEMBER

A local expert in bells, Vincent Aguillon, is visiting Purnon to update the inventory of the region's historic bells. The oldest fixed object on the property is, surprisingly, the bell that sits above the chapel. It dates from 1661, which makes it more than a hundred years older than the château. It's independently listed as a *monument historique*. We are intrigued to learn that it arrived at Purnon long after the château was built, during the Montesquiou-Fézensac era. Vincent carefully photographs it, measures its dimensions, notes the motifs of the armorial features and even an image of the Virgin on the bell. He then makes a recording of the bell chiming, which Flick and I hear for the first time.

I ask him if he would like to see our other bells. He checks his records and is somewhat surprised. There are others? We take him first to the entrance of the stables. And then to the 1812 gate. This bell has been struck individually rather than from a mould and is certainly original. Vincent notices that it is not secured in any way and could be stolen, so we take it inside until we can properly attach it. Next we pass by the eastern wall of the château where the beautiful bell that Pierre recalled summoning children to lunch still sits. Vincent mounts the scaffolding, which affords a closer view. It's a bell struck by the Fonderie de Amédée Bollée in Le Mans, Sarthe. Its wooden mount is badly rotted, but the bell itself is in wonderful condition. We head inside and four more bells that we have found around the château are produced for Vincent's inspection. Fleurs-de-lis suggest one dates from before the Revolution. We also show him several that are still in place in various rooms from the château's old system for summoning domestic staff.

Left: The chapel bell. The oldest fixed object on the domain.
Centre: Reminders of class distinctions are everywhere at Purnon. This bell, used for summoning domestic staff, sits in a tiny *entresol* above a finely decorated dressing room.

23 NOVEMBER

It's called imposter syndrome – the fear that our lack of qualifications will expose us as frauds. Elected to local council at the age of nineteen and then a government minister at age thirty, it's been a lifelong affliction for me. Now, surrounded by power tools and agricultural equipment that I'm still mastering, in a language I'm still learning, and working on an immense project for which I have precisely no experience, I am acutely tormented.

We lack any obvious DIY skills – carpentry, plumbing, electricity. Even the outdoor tools and machinery were new to us when we arrived. While we are learning fast, mistakes and frustrations are frequent. We struggle to solve problems that more practically minded people would solve in an instant.

But we are learning to leverage our existing skills in innovative ways.

Flick is a marketing genius. Our Instagram and Facebook accounts are growing rapidly. The content is original and engaging. Through social media, our sales of slate drink coasters and other merchandise and donations are climbing.

Our YouTube channel is now earning revenue. It's a virtuous circle. We enjoy making content that enables us to share our journey with enthusiasts around the world, and now every view is generating income to support the château's restoration.

We have teamed up with French documentary program *Grands Reportages* on the TF1 network to showcase our journey restoring a bedroom and bathroom on the first floor. Flick has offered the opportunity to collaborate with us on the project to a high-end paint and wallpaper manufacturer, Farrow & Ball. It's great exposure for them on an iconic project and a wonderful opportunity for us to access elegant materials that would have stretched our limited budget. Other partnerships soon follow – bathroom fittings and bed and bathroom linen. A Skydio drone arrives and revolutionises our filming, and a steady supply of clothes from the iconic Australian workwear brand, Hard Yakka, stems the staggering rate at which we have been consuming gear. We may be novices with the tools but we're finding other ways to exploit our previous talents.

We lack any obvious DIY skills – carpentry, plumbing, electricity … but we are learning to leverage our existing skills in innovative ways.

On our journey to save Purnon we are surrounded by beauty and challenges.

24 NOVEMBER

The scaffolding now towers fourteen metres above the château, divided across seven levels. Loïc from Soporen declares it safe enough for us to accompany him on a tour. For the first time we see the upper parts of our stonework and roof up close. I wasn't prepared for just how much it had deteriorated. The soft stone around the dormers is flaking away and comes off in your hand at the slightest touch. Many of the tiles are broken or have shifted, others have fallen. We spot the telltale signs of silicone on tiles that have been replaced haphazardly in more recent times.

The zinc guttering system added at the end of the nineteenth century altered the pitch of the roof, substantially changing its appearance. The stage one works include an ambitious project to remove that system and rebuild the wooden frame to its original shape.

25 NOVEMBER

The scaffolding affords a once in a lifetime opportunity to view the huge *blazons* (coats of arms) that are nestled in the pediments above the front and rear entrances to the château.

The two shields contain the coats of arms of Monsieur Achard de la Haye and his wife, Madame Bénigne-Modeste de la Motte-Baracé, with a marquis coronet towering above. Laurels and weapons signify Monsieur Achard de la Haye's military career. Each shield bears a rampant lion.

Colours are represented by lines (horizontal for azure, vertical for red). Merlettes (beakless birds) and fleurs-de-lis decorate the arms of madame. At the base we can clearly see the cross of the Ordre de Saint-Louis, a royal decoration typically given to officers upon their retirement.

The two coats of arms presented in this fashion symbolise their marriage in 1767, just before the purchase of the estate upon which they would build Château de Purnon.

It is remarkable to see the heraldic symbols so closely. Thankfully, despite requiring a careful clean, they appear to be in excellent condition.

15 DECEMBER

Philippe and Greg arrive to film the first instalment of the French heritage documentary. As well as the usual elements regarding the stage one works and the history of Purnon, the documentary will follow Flick and me as we restore a bedroom and bathroom on the first floor in preparation for the arrival of Flick's parents next April. The deadline is somewhat intimidating as we reflect on all the tasks that will need to be completed for the rooms to be ready. Experience has taught us that despite our planning, there are always nasty surprises and unanticipated discoveries.

24 DECEMBER

Christmas Eve dinner with José and Blanche at their home. It's hard to believe that a year has passed since we hosted them for Christmas lunch. We've worked so hard and achieved so much with our growing band of volunteers, and we have great plans for the year ahead.

25 DECEMBER

Christmas lunch with a wonderful friend, Crispin, in Richelieu. We are promised turkey with all the trimmings and we're sold. It's wonderful to relax in a beautifully restored *maison bourgeoise* (yes, that's what a large private dwelling in a town centre is called!). We enjoy the warmth both physically and metaphorically.

Richelieu is our favourite local town. It's named after the famed French statesman Cardinal Richelieu (1585-1642), whose grand château sat on a vast estate just nearby. He was chief minister to Louis XIII and is a towering figure in French history.

The château is sadly gone - demolished for building materials in 1805. However, its remarkable grounds can still be enjoyed.

Having built his château, Cardinal Richelieu also ordered the construction of a model town, laid out on a grid and surrounded by moats. The resulting town of Richelieu has charm along with its fascinating history, and we love visiting and strolling its streets.

First-time visitors to the château are surprised to discover that the zinc guttering at the base of the roof is not original. It was added at the end of the nineteenth century and required a substantial change to the pitch of the roof.

THE TWO COATS OF ARMS
SYMBOLISE THEIR MARRIAGE
IN 1767, JUST BEFORE THE
PURCHASE OF THE ESTATE
UPON WHICH THEY WOULD
BUILD CHÂTEAU DE PURNON.

29 DECEMBER

We're shocked and concerned about the dampness we're finding inside the château. It's been raining constantly. Despite the plastic sheeting on the floor of much of the *grenier*, we're still emptying hundreds of litres of water out of windows from the buckets scattered strategically about. But we're now observing increasing condensation throughout the unheated parts of the château. It's in the *grand salon* and the *bibliothèque*, and the walls of the corridors in the *sous-sol* (basement) are dripping wet. It seems far worse than we recall from last year. The unmistakable black discolouration of mould is appearing on the walls of the second floor. It's a threat to both the château and our health. We need the stage one works to progress in order to seal the château.

Centre: Plastic sheets and makeshift containers are never enough when heavy rains overpower our leaky roof.
Right: We're desperate for the major works to progress so that we can start to tackle condensation throughout the château.

30 DECEMBER

A clear and crisp winter's day, perfect for the hunting *rallye*. As the sun sets, the hunters return from the forest. We've been invited to share in the post-hunt activities known as *la curée* at Les Petits Fougets, a modest farm that serves as a hunting lodge just on the forest edge. The hounds are rewarded for their work and the dead animals are honoured.

They've shot five *sangliers* and a *chevreuil*. The carcasses are suspended on hooks in the abattoir. Pierre de Rochequairie emerges with an apron and a boning knife. I have to admit that my respect for him grows as I observe him expertly butchering the animals. An electric saw neatly decapitates the *chevreuil* – yes, they've literally killed Bambi. The blood is washed away.

Nearby, children are chasing each other in play and the adults regale one other with growing tales of the day's adventures. It appears that Pierre's son-in-law, Vladimir, dispatched the largest of the *sangliers* at over 120 kilograms. He is clearly very chuffed.

There are about twenty licensed hunters permitted to shoot and a very strict quota of which animals and how many can be shot on any particular day. Many others are part of the day's activities - observing, securing the area to protect unwitting members of the general public, and buglers who signal the results after shots are fired. Each *rallye* has its own badges and bugle calls. It's a tradition that has been passed down over many generations. I'm surprised by the social diversity, the number of women and the presence of children.

All of the meat is collected and distributed.

It is hard to imagine Purnon without hunting, situated as it is on the edge of the magnificent Forêt de Scévolles. It's an ancient tradition and nowadays a controversial one. But it is impossible to comprehend the lives of the people in our local community without understanding hunting.

Traditionally, nobles hunted with packs of trained hounds. This form of hunting is known as *la vénerie* or *chasse à courre*. Smaller animals could be hunted on foot - hares, foxes or rabbits - while *chevreuils*, *cerfs* or *sangliers* were often hunted on horseback. Even today, there are around 390 hunting teams across France, of which 172 hunt on horseback. The dogs are specially bred for their endurance, incredible sense of smell and ability to live and work as a team.

The first hunting team connected with Purnon was l'Équipage de la Ratellerie. It was established by General Canuel in 1810 with his colleagues Monsieur Achard de la Haye, Monsieur Confex-Lachambre (then mayor of Loudun) and Monsieur du Petit Thours. General Canuel had been a celebrated French soldier during the Revolutionary Wars but later became a fervent supporter of the Bourbon Restoration. They hunted in the Forêt de Scévolles and in the forests around Chinon. This team was wound up in 1816.

Édouard Achard, Marquis de la Haye created a new team in 1820 known as the Rallye-Scévolles. They hunted wolves (*loups*), *cerfs* and later *chevreuils*. Upon the marquis' death in 1844, the leadership of the *rallye* passed (along with the château) to the Baron de Goyon, his son-in-law. Then, with the death of the Baron de Goyon in 1851, it passed to the Comte Fernand de Montesquiou-Fézensac, who would lead the team until 1867. They wore a green jacket with red trimmings. The Rallye-Scévolles then joined with the Rallye-Monnoie. This team, which was closely connected with the famed French cavalry school at Saumur, hunted in the forest of Crémille in Touraine and was dissolved in 1885.

Soon Purnon would be purchased by the de Rochequairie family. The Comte de Rochequairie (as he was then) led the Rallye-Guérinière. It was so named as the dogs were kennelled at La Guérinière at the western end of the Scévolles forest. Sadly, the magnificent old kennels have been destroyed and we have only a late-nineteenth-century photo to show us how they looked.

The Comte de Rochequairie was the *maître d'équipage* (literally the master of the team) from 1877 to 1905. He was known as an intrepid rider and a great hunter. The team hunted in the Forêt de Scévolles and the park at the Château d'Oiron (as the Comte d'Oyron was his father-in-law). They had a pack of around sixty hounds and wore a blue jacket with red trim. When we arrived at Purnon, Flick rescued one of the uniforms from a huge chest in the attic.

The Rallye-Loudun was created in 1866 by the Comte d'Oyron. In about 1888 he left the *rallye* to its younger hunters and joined his fourteen hunting dogs to the Rallye-Guérinière.

The tradition has been passed through many generations. In our community it touches people of all ages and social classes.

It is hard to imagine Purnon without hunting, situated as it is on the edge of the magnificent Forêt de Scévolles. It's an ancient tradition and nowadays a controversial one. But it is impossible to comprehend the lives of the people in our local community without understanding hunting.

Right: Our terracotta deer linking Purnon's hunting past with the contemporary lives of the people who live in our community.
Following page: A trophy from an earlier hunt – a stag from perhaps a century ago.

31 DECEMBER

It's our second New Year's Eve at Purnon. We work on the bedroom and bathroom restoration during the day and then we're off to Kate, Benji and Izzy's home for Saint-Sylvestre celebrations. Flick comes from a large family with many siblings. She instantly warms to the noise and banter of their adult children, several of whom we are meeting for the first time. It's a wonderful and relaxing evening after a year of demanding work.

4 JANUARY

A nightmare has ended.

On Sunday, the château's Instagram was successfully hacked, the password lifted and the account hijacked. The hacker demanded a ransom, a modest sum in bitcoin. We immediately sought to access Instagram and Facebook's security systems for retrieving stolen or hacked accounts. We were shocked at how indifferent and impenetrable their security service proved.

The hacker gave us two days to pay or the account would be deleted and everything irretrievably lost.

We set to work copying as much of the content as we could as quickly as possible. The loss of the account with its tens of thousands of followers who we have painstakingly amassed over almost two years would be a disaster.

We attempted to escalate the matter within Instagram. We contacted a friend with high-level access who raised the matter with a Facebook vice-president. We heard nothing.

After two days and having negotiated the ransom down, we pay. We are crushed at having financed cybercrime, but with no response from Instagram, we were left with no option. The hacker sends tips to ensure that our account is more secure and signs the message off with a heart emoji - I almost admire her chutzpah. In a clear case of Stockholm syndrome, we end up loathing Instagram more than the hacker.

And we have learned a brutal lesson.

13 JANUARY

The restoration of the château façades is now in full swing. The *tuffeau* stones have all been individually assessed. Those to be replaced have been chalked with red crosses and those that require restoration have been marked in blue. The limestone render and the remaining stones are being delicately cleaned by hand using small brushes and an anti-mould treatment. The black stains disappear and the exquisite original hue returns. It's stunning to watch our château gradually returning to its original tones of yellow and white.

The stonemasons set to work on the château façades.

14 JANUARY

I'm home alone. Flick has returned briefly to Australia for the first time in almost two years.

This week I've been enveloped by our coldest weather since we arrived. The mercury has plunged to minus six degrees Celsius and some days it never gets above zero. I notice an icy chill in the small part of the château where we live. A touch of the radiator immediately confirms my fear - our heating has stopped.

We have two large tanks that hold two thousand litres of heating fuel. They are somewhat antiquated, and to keep tabs on our consumption I'm required to use an old wooden dipstick. It's hard to tell how quickly they are emptying. Of course, I've hopelessly misjudged when we would run out. I'll have to wait two weeks for the next delivery. We order our fuel through a cooperative of locals - a couple of bulk orders each year keeps the price down for everyone. The château gets colder every day as the retained heat disappears. Truffe looks at me with obvious disapproval. Her expression says it all: the château was so much warmer when Flick was here!

At least I can spare Flick the consequences of my lack of foresight. Soon I'm eating lunch and dinner wearing a scarf, beanie and gloves.

My original dreams of château life never included winter. I imagined long days, warm nights, working outdoors with the château basking in never-ending sunshine. I secretly feared the dark and drab winter. In truth, winter brings its own ghostly beauty.

The first thing I notice is the silence - a complete silence on deathly still days. The distant sounds of farming disappear. Any hint of life in the village recedes. The rustle of autumnal leaves is gone. Just silence.

In the morning, mist clings to the landscape. The *grand allée*, the forest, the 1812 gate and sometimes even the *cour d'honneur* are swallowed up. The pervading sense of profound isolation is both eerie and peaceful. On these mornings, the silence seems somehow deeper.

With the temperature below zero, the prairie freezes and turns a powdery soft white, the trees all dusted with ice.

On some days the fog never lifts and we spend the day cocooned from the world around us. But often the sun pushes through, the fog clears and suddenly blue skies afford an incredible view of the white forest spreading all around us.

The trees, many now devoid of their leaves, take on a mysterious, haunting look. By late afternoon the sun dips below the Éolienne Bollée and the sky glows orange.

Centre: The sun dips over the Éolienne Bollée.
Right: The winter mist swallows the *grand allée*.

*The pervading sense of profound isolation
is both eerie and peaceful.*

24 JANUARY

Monsieur Didier is here for a site visit to inspect the progress so far. The various companies assemble and outline the work they have completed. The schedule is starting to slip and Monsieur Didier gives them a rev-up. The scaffolding is the single largest expense. It provides a shared platform for all the various trades, so it's necessary for them to progress at a similar pace so it can be moved to the second half of the château later in the year. No one can fall behind.

26 JANUARY

Flick has returned from her visit to Australia. Her displeasure at the igloo that awaits is obvious.

It seems like an ideal time to do a few field trips in the warm car. Our first excursion takes us to the Royal Abbey at nearby Fontevraud. This incredible edifice, founded in 1101, was the final resting place of Eleanor of Aquitaine, her second husband, Henry II, King of England, one of her sons, Richard the Lionheart, and his brother's second wife, Isabella of Angoulême. The four recumbent statues (known as *gisant* in French) lie sombrely in the otherwise deserted abbey. Their actual remains were scattered during the Revolution. In the nineteenth and twentieth centuries, the abbey became one of France's harshest prisons. Today it has been comprehensively restored, and the old stables house an impressive modern art collection.

27 JANUARY

Today we've escaped to Angers to collect an original Louis XVI *canapé* (sofa) that Flick has purchased at on online antique auction. While furnishing our Paris apartment, we learned to tell the difference between 'epoch' (an original item of furniture) and 'style' (in the spirit of the era depicted but a nineteenth- or twentieth-century replica). The replicas, while perfectly nice to look at, are rarely as valuable.

There's always a little nervousness collecting something you've bought sight unseen. Our hearts soar - the *canapé* is magnificent and in wonderful condition.

Left: Each evening we mount the scaffolding to view
the day's progress.
Following page: The Louis XVI *canapé* finds a place in our
unrestored *grand salon*.

28 JANUARY

Today we welcome Monsieur Didier Gautier to Purnon. He is a retired restorer of pianos.

When we purchased the château, the *bibliothèque* was home to a decaying grand piano forsaken by the de Rochequairie family, doubtless because it would have been impossible to move.

It's an Érard, a prestigious Parisian brand founded in 1780. Thanks to Flick's siblings it has now been tuned twice and plays decently. We've located the serial number and a search online reveals that it dates from 1860. Our excitement upon identifying this is tempered by the reality that grand pianos are basically worthless upon reaching a certain age - the thousands of moving parts make restoration uneconomical and its old wooden frame will make it difficult to tune regularly. But with boxes of sheet music dating back to before the Revolution, it strikes a sentimental chord - we will endeavour to restore it.

After a careful inspection, Monsieur Gautier declares himself confident that the piano can be restored and says he will take it on for us. Several parts will need to be taken away and repaired in his workshop, and some of the badly degraded wood must be completely replaced.

With boxes of sheet music dating back to before the Revolution, it strikes a sentimental chord – we will endeavour to restore it.

The *bibliothèque* – home to our Érard grand piano.

31 JANUARY

Finally, we have heating back!

After the fuel delivery on Friday morning, we were ready to feel warmth again. But when we turned on the boiler in the basement that heats our radiators … *rien*. Nothing! We couldn't believe it. After a frustrating hour troubleshooting, we called our heating guy. He's here by early afternoon and gives the boiler a thorough clean, but it still won't start. A broken transformer is identified as the culprit, but by now it's impossible to get a new one before everything closes on Friday for the weekend.

The news that we will be without heating for another two days falls heavily on Flick. She has soldiered through the frozen château since her return, but this turn of events is too cruel. Tears are shed. Sometimes we can endure almost any discomfort, but there is a breaking point, and when it's reached, we each in turn must play the role of picking the other up.

Sometimes we can endure almost any discomfort, but there is a breaking point, and when it's reached, we each in turn must play the role of picking the other up.

1 FEBRUARY

And just like that, our roof is disappearing before our eyes. In a single day, the FP Couverture team has removed thousands of *ardoise* tiles and many of the wooden battens that support them. Only the *charpente* remains on one huge section of roof. In the late afternoon we stand in the *grenier* and can see for miles around us. With daylight now flooding in, we start to notice things that the darkness had concealed. The graffiti on the stone chimney columns becomes clearer. Pieces of the frame that have become disconnected from others – possibly causing the wave effect discernible in parts of the roof – become visible. The removal of some lower sections of the roof reveals masonry walls that were concealed beneath it. The incredible workmanship involved in constructing the massive interlocking wooden frame that supported the tiled roof is visible for us to admire against a blue sky and a fast-setting sun. It is breathtaking.

The team leads us to a section of the second-floor ceiling. Above it was one of the worst and most persistent leaks in the *grenier*. The huge load-bearing wooden beam is almost completely rotted through. It's a risk to anyone walking in that section of the *grenier* and will need to be quickly addressed through a temporary support. It's another reminder that our stage one works are occurring just in the nick of time.

AND JUST LIKE THAT,
OUR ROOF IS DISAPPEARING
BEFORE OUR EYES.

2 FEBRUARY

We are making great progress on the first-floor bedroom and bathroom.

The wallpaper and its *toile de jute* backing and the wooden frames that supported the wallpaper panels have all come down. Many thousands of small tacks have been removed and the ceiling sanded and plastered. A mist primer is applied.

The *boiseries* (panelling) are scrubbed and filled in preparation for undercoating and painting.

Flick has been working with Farrow & Ball to select the right colour combination from their elegant collection of handcrafted wallpapers and paints.

This week we have the assistance of Olympia, the daughter of a friend from nearby Saumur. For her work experience week at school she has chosen to work here at Purnon. She proves a whiz at plastering.

But as we remove the old bathroom fittings, the results of a leaky toilet and bath start to become apparent. The wooden parquetry is completely rotted in the north-west corner of the room. As we lift the damaged floor we notice the impact on the joists and wooden beams underneath. The damage is significant: we can see right through to the room below.

We head down to the *entresol*, mount the narrow staircase and stare at the ceiling. It's a disaster. In several places the beam has completely rotted through. There is no way we can place a bath on the floor above it.

We seek the expert advice of the team from Métiers du Bois who are working on the roof *charpente*. They quickly identify the extent of the rotted beams - several must be replaced in part or in whole. It won't be cheap, but at least they are already on site with the expertise and the right tools.

5 FEBRUARY

After a day working on the bedroom and bathroom restoration, we're off to dinner at the home of Bruno Belin in Monts-sur-Guesnes.

Bruno is our local pharmacist. He is also a member of the French Senate. My political brain goes into overdrive, digesting the various roles that the French political system allows him to hold simultaneously. He is a local councillor in the commune of Monts-sur-Guesnes, an elected representative to the Departmental Council of Vienne and a delegate to the committee that runs the Pays Loudunais region.

Bruno embodies the oft-cited maxim that all politics is local. He is a great supporter of preserving local heritage. In that role he has driven the restoration of the immense medieval château at Monts-sur-Guesnes and its conversion into a *historial* (a form of museum) that will showcase Middle Ages history.

Bruno has converted a space next to his pharmacy in the heart of the village into a museum about the history of the pharmacy profession. It's surprisingly interesting. We've been scouring the château for old medicine bottles that bear the inscription of the Monts-sur-Guesnes pharmacy. We've found a few, and just before we sit down to dinner we present them to Bruno. He disappears and returns moments later with beautifully bound prescription books dating back to the turn of the twentieth century. He uses the potion numbers on the bottles to identify the various concoctions and the ailments they would have treated.

Bruno is also a great source of encouragement for our mission to save Purnon. He has enormous energy and intuitively understands the value to the broader region of the investment that we are making in its restoration.

The dinner is also an opportunity to get an update on the works at the Monts-sur-Guesnes château, which should open in May.

Flick details the *boiseries* in the first-floor bedroom.

8 FEBRUARY

Monsieur Didier is on site with all of the workers to check progress. The team from Direction Régionale des Affaires Culturelles (DRAC) is also bringing the head of the region to view the project for the first time – his support is vital if French government funding is to continue for future phases. With all the activity, the documentary crew is returning to film our progress on the bedroom and bathroom.

Flick is unwell and confined to bed. Mademoiselle Truffe proves a sympathetic nurse.

The regional head of DRAC, Monsieur Bourel le Guilloux arrives with Madame Bordeau and the rest of the team. The weather smiles on us, a crisp, sunny day with brilliant blue skies. Monsieur Didier conducts an enthusiastic tour of the property. It's a joy to hear him explain Purnon to a specialist audience. After several hours, we gather for refreshments in the *salle à manger*. There's a lot riding on the meeting. Without the financial support of the French government, future tranches of the restoration will become impossible. I try to convey our passion and energy in my broken French. I wish Flick was here.

They love the project and wish to extend heritage protection to further buildings across the domain – the *orangerie* and the *chai* are mentioned. There is even discussion of including original furnishings such as the billiard table and the old carriage abandoned in the *chai*. This is a good sign, but the conversation is taking an unfortunate turn. Clearly the fiscal situation at DRAC is tight. There is no escaping the bad news that Monsieur Bourel le Guilloux is delivering: the level of DRAC funding for the second tranche will be lower. It's a terrible blow.

I put on a brave face for the documentary crew. The team who will restore our royal busts for the roof arrive to carefully crate the stone pieces away. I wonder how we will afford all the elements of our restoration plans.

15 FEBRUARY

It's still dark when we awake, and a full moon illuminates the sky. We have a two-hour drive to reach the Déballage Marchand Le Mans, an enormous *brocante* (antique market) in Le Mans. It's for professional traders only but we've been able to obtain an access card because of our work at Purnon.

As the sun rises above the Le Mans exhibition grounds, the track of the legendary twenty-four-hour automobile race emerges before us. Although not due to open officially until 8 am, the bargain hunters are already rifling through trucks and trailers by torchlight. This is not the place for idle flâneurs or for those looking for a couple of candlesticks for the lounge room. It's serious business as professional antique dealers ruthlessly race to snatch up the best bargains in the first hours. Just about every vehicle in the parking lot is a truck or a car towing a trailer so that loot can be hauled away. The prices are very competitive, and it's basically cash only for most of the merchants.

Hunting for bargain antiques has to be one of the great joys of living in France. In Paris, Flick and I idled away weekends at the Marché aux Puces in Saint-Ouen. Decorating our Paris apartment became an apprenticeship in recognising the various eras of French design and furnishings. We became friendly with some of the characters who sell to the tourists flocking each week to Europe's largest flea market.

One flamboyant gentleman with a striking silver mane touched with a vaguely purple tinge we nicknamed Monsieur Discount. He had a disconcerting habit of commencing every negotiation by consulting a tiny book filled with an illegible handwritten scrawl, then quoting an outrageous initial price. He would then immediately discount it by as much as seventy or eighty per cent – a discount, we were assured, just for us. It was from this point that the negotiations could actually commence. We purchased a couple of items from Monsieur Discount – a console, a Napoleon III table – and were well satisfied. Then one afternoon, after several hours of tense negotiations, we successfully landed an elegant Louis XV commode. He was thrilled and presented us with a bottle of champagne. Our disappointment at realising that we must have shockingly overpaid somewhat soured the taste of the bubbles!

From the Marché aux Puces we progressed to the Drouot auction house, another venerable Paris institution. The auctions are conducted with lightning speed and it's easy for the inexperienced to become confused. Once, while bidding for a stunning Empire mirror, the auctioneer took pity upon me and pointed out to the amused assembled throng that I was, in fact, bidding against myself. Needless to say, the mirror now graces one of our bedrooms!

Today in Le Mans we're on the hunt for Louis XVI furnishings for the bedroom and bathroom that we are restoring on the first floor – mirrors, *appliques* (wall lights), side tables, chandeliers and a bed. The range is colossal, and with hard bargaining we secure several items.

Right: The de Rochequairie coat of arms adorns one of the huge wine vats in our *chai*.
Following page: Mirrors from our antique hunting, destined for future restored rooms.

Today the Soporen team is accompanying us on a visit to the *tuffeau* quarry at Marigny-Brizay, which will be the source for the stone used to restore the château façades.

Tuffeau is a limestone indigenous to our part of the Loire Valley. It's soft and light with a very low density and thus easy for masons to shape. Almost all of the châteaux in our region are constructed from *tuffeau* stone.

Centuries of mining have created extensive networks of underground quarries. Throughout our region, communities of troglodytes inhabited these tunnels. Today, some are used for growing mushrooms, as their darkness and constant temperature create ideal conditions for cultivation.

We descend hundreds of metres underground along an access tunnel into the *carrière* (quarry) and finally arrive at the colossal blocks that have been cut for Purnon. Some weigh over five tonnes. The blocks have been individually numbered with markings to indicate colour, weight, condition and even their exact orientation within the chamber from which they have been cut. We can see the enormous industrial cutting vehicles at work extracting the stone blocks with massive chainsaws. It's hard to imagine how the stone was quarried and transported centuries ago without the equipment that is mobilised today.

In the evening we attend the *assemblée générale du comité des fêtes* of Verrue. It's effectively the annual meeting for Verrue residents to elect the committee that organises the major social gatherings in the village. Despite the chill, twenty-two people assemble in Verrue's *salle des fêtes*.

The meeting kicks off with a quick recap of the events of the previous year, 14 July celebrations and a Halloween parade for the village children. But the meeting quickly descends into procedural pandemonium as the election is conducted. Some nominate by proxy, with family and friends calling out their names. Certain office-holders must leave the room while the voting by show of hands is conducted. A mobile phone rings and the meeting is interrupted while a disorientated villager is directed to the venue. The voting rules are unfathomable to Flick and me; at some points we are allowed to vote and at others we are prevented. But amidst the shambolic chaos, a friendly congeniality pervades the room.

We finish with a glass of wine and then everyone disappears into the darkness.

Tuffeau *is a limestone indigenous to our part of the Loire Valley. It's soft and light with a very low density and thus easy for masons to shape.*

Proverbes
L'amour est aveugle

21 FEBRUARY

Two days of high winds have badly damaged the massive tarpaulins that protect sections of our roof where the tiles have been removed. The winds have also smashed the temporary lights that the *charpente* team set up in the *grenier* for their workshop. Progress feels painstakingly slow.

24 FEBRUARY

Pierre and his granddaughter Agathe drop by to view the works so far. After coffee, we show them our progress on the first-floor bedroom. Pierre recalls that it was his parents' room. While removing the wall coverings we discovered chalked graffiti underneath from the painter of the *boiseries* in 1911: *'pour le marquis de la Rochequairie'*. Pierre is horrified by the incorrect rendering of the de Rochequairie name. And so this attribution, which has laid hidden for over a hundred and ten years, is corrected in an instant as Pierre's thumb removes the extraneous *'la'*!

We head upstairs to check progress on the roof. Rummaging around the *grenier*, Agathe comes upon a small collection of scraps that have survived the earlier purge. Beneath a couple of broken picture frames destined for the tip she uncovers an exquisite drawing. We move it into the light. It needs a good dust but we can see that it's a striking sketch of a heroic figure from antiquity that bears the handwritten inscription 'Purnon, December 1824'. The figure is marked Ephestion (Hephaestion in English), the Macedonian nobleman and lifelong friend of Alexander the Great.

4 MARCH

After a week of frenzied activity, it really feels that we are making substantial progress on several of our projects.

On Monday, the Métiers du Bois team sets to work fixing the rotted beams under the bathroom floor. In three days, they're done.

At the same time, Monsieur Gautier commences work on the restoration of the Érard piano. It will be an intricate and time-consuming task, but his efforts on the woodwork yield immediate and promising results. The pedal box is in a terrible state. Parts of it will need to be completely remodelled. But the hammers and tuning pins appear serviceable.

The tiles are being taken off the roof, dropping into a huge hopper with a swoosh and a crash after descending fourteen metres through the debris chute. The current roof comprises a blend of badly worn original tiles combined with some later replacements. For both practical and aesthetic reasons, none can be retained. We rescue some of the better ones for our slate coasters. The work restoring the *charpente* can progress as the tiles are lifted.

On Wednesday, a massive day of clearing in the *bois* with the tractor. Fallen partly rotted tree trunks are cut and burned. The better wood is delivered to neighbours for heating. Old stumps are ripped out. We move several large concrete troughs that posed a hazard to tractors. Local farmers cut and bale the hay and lucerne in our prairies in the late spring. Now that I've cleared the fencing, fewer hazards will make it quicker and safer for them to work across the estate.

Clearing in the woods near the *pavillon de potager* yields a curious discovery. I come across one half of a stone sphere covered in moss and buried in the ground, an indentation suggesting the original sphere must have been mounted on a metal *piquet*. It looks vaguely familiar, and I suddenly recall that I came across the other half buried in the *douve sèche* (dry moat). José points up at the *ardoise* roof of the pavilion. Sure enough, a metal *piquet* that I had never noticed before sits on top. The mystery is solved – the stone sphere would have been perched at the apex of the conical roof. I reunite the two halves and await Monsieur Didier's arrival on Monday to show him our latest find.

5 MARCH

Dinner with a wonderful couple, Pierre and Axelle de Feydeau, at their home, the Château de la Tour-de-Ry. Younger than us, they have completely restored a château dating from the last quarter of the fifteenth century. It was in ruins when they acquired it.

The château is a complete contrast to Purnon. It still retains many defensive elements and some of its decorative features typify the earlier Renaissance period. We ascend a staircase in one of their towers to view fragments of frescoes dating from the construction of the château.

Catching up with Pierre and Axelle always gives us a lift. Pierre comes from a French family passionate about preserving heritage, and his father, Bertrand, has been a great supporter of Purnon's restoration project. They regale us with stories of their own restoration journey, including an episode that saw a massive stone building collapse into their moat. It was probably less amusing at the time! It's an anecdote significantly enhanced by the realisation that the restored building has become the spectacular room where we are dining.

Clockwise from top left:
Hephaestion sketched at Purnon in 1822 and found
in the attic exactly two centuries later.
The ground floor.
Intimate letters found hidden in the small bureau.
Shoes and fabrics from the château's past.

7 MARCH

Shopping at local markets is one of the many pleasures of life in France. Our favourite is in the nearby town of Lencloître on the first Monday of each month.

There's always a dazzling array of local seasonal produce. Succulent peaches and nectarines. Sweet meringues, crumbling on the outside and with a soft, luscious centre. Oysters from Bretagne, shucked in front of you so that you can inhale them on the spot. Eels are grilled on hot coals and the aroma wafts across the market. Huge spears of the most delicious green asparagus I've ever tasted. Hundreds of varieties of cow and goat cheeses. Apple ciders, cured meats, locally cultivated honey, regional mustards. More varieties of mushrooms than I ever knew existed. Terrines, bread and eye-watering *pâtisserie*. All of it impeccably presented.

It's France, so the correct social etiquette must be observed.

Never touch the fresh fruit and vegetables. The grocer selects the choicest pieces for you, and then weighs and bags them.

At the butcher, no French person orders meat by weight. You indicate what you are cooking and for how many adults and children. It's the butcher's job to select the most appropriate cuts of meat and the required quantity. On the occasions where we have violated these rules, chaos has ensued.

Eight hundred grams of prosciutto, please.
What for?
Pizza.
How many people?
Umm ... Four. I can feel my confidence evaporating.
That's too much, he replies implacably.
I like prosciutto, I say weakly.
Two hundred grams per adult – it's too much.
Perhaps they're large pizzas, another customer helpfully intercedes. I nod gratefully.
What else is going on the pizza? The butcher asks forensically.

I can feel impatience rising from the customers around me. Is it with me or him? Finally he gives in and hands it over disdainfully. It's a pyrrhic victory. Will I ever be allowed to shop at that stall again?

SHOPPING AT LOCAL MARKETS IS ONE OF THE MANY PLEASURES OF LIFE IN FRANCE.

ici
c'est
TROP
BON

Clementines
5,00€ les 3 kilo

E SAU
Saucisson
- Porc Poc
- Poivre
- Herbe
- Fumé
- Noisette
- Tomate séchée
- Figues
- Chorizo
- Ail des Ours
- Camembert
- Comté
- Fromage de chèvre
- Bleu d'A

9 MARCH

Purnon's immense basements are a window into an era when armies of people served the wealthy.

As well as the two large kitchens for the preparation and cooking of the extravagant food that would have once been served in the *salle à manger*, smaller rooms give a hint of the food storage challenges of an age without refrigeration.

In one room, a large cage is suspended from the ceiling. It would have held cheeses and dried meats and kept them safe from rodents. The *monte-plats* just needs its rope replaced and the pulley system could again enable plates to ascend to the ground floor for serving.

In another room we find an old latrine, complete with a porcelain-handled manual flush mechanism.

One room, with a stubborn door that we must force open, contains piles of charcoal briquettes along with shovels and buckets. Eerily, as though someone walked away mid-task, the room lay abandoned and untouched for perhaps a century until we came upon it again.

In a space that sits directly under the bridge at the back of the château we come across a decaying longcase clock and a charming freestanding bath from an era before plumbing. It would have been filled by hand.

Two enormous heaters (*calorifères*) were installed in basement corridors at the end of the nineteenth century to act as a central heating system connected by huge ducts to many of the rooms on the ground floor and the corridor of the first floor. The huge cast-iron system was encased in locally fired bricks from the Milleron brick factory. Parts of the original brick factory and its chimney still sit close by in the Scévolles forest and are protected as *monuments historiques*.

Although not particularly ugly, the two heaters and the ducts are in a state of disrepair and probably haven't heated the château for close to a hundred years. In several places, the removal of this system will allow us to admire the huge stone vaults of the basement ceiling. As the heaters are not original, our architect is happy for us to remove them. José and I set to work on the smaller one. Alain Costa will recycle the bricks, on which the local inscription is still visible. The cast iron has a modest scrap value so we take it to be recycled. We come across the remnants of two old packets of Gold Flake cigarettes from Bristol in the UK. The packaging helps us to ascertain that the heaters probably haven't been used since around the 1930s.

Everything has to be dragged out of the basement and taken in wheelbarrows through the tunnels to our trailer. It takes us almost two days, but the visual impact is immediate. I can't wait to tackle the other much more prominent heater.

10 MARCH

Flick is away, so José hosts dinner at his home.

It's a great boys' night in. José has prepared foie gras followed by freshly shucked oysters. I supply a muscadet to accompany the oysters and his cousin brings a Paris-Brest pastry for dessert. Detailed discussions enliven each course – which local market has the best oysters, the exact method for preparing a Belgian endive salad, which pâtisserie makes the best version of a particular French gâteau.

In a country obsessed with food, people hold strong opinions and defend them enthusiastically. The exact temperature at which to cook a *tarte vigneronne aux pommes* (a specialty of nearby Chinon) is the subject of forensic debate.

Right: These small cupboards were for storing the
personal effects of the staff who worked (and often lived)
in Purnon's basement.
Following page left to right:
An old fromager for storing cheese.
In a forgotten corner of the basement a bath and pram
lie abandoned.

Left: The coal cellar.
Above: The kitchen's original fireplace.

11 MARCH

This week saw the first deliveries of our new stone for the façade restoration. The more complex shapes will be prepared to exact measurements at the Soporen workshop. The simple cuts can be done with chainsaws and by hand here at the château. The stone blocks are unloaded and the masons set to work. Progress is surprisingly fast as the *tuffeau* stone is soft and supple. Our *lucarnes* (dormers) on the second floor are rapidly transformed. With great expertise, degraded stone blocks are removed while temporary supports hold the remaining pieces in place. As if balancing a giant house of cards, the stonemasons must slip the lower stones out without compromising the structure around them. Meanwhile, the team from Métiers du Bois is making great progress on the *charpente*. They must correct a significant deformation in the roofline that appears like a giant wave. Oak supports are fixed in place. The carpenters must also adjust the roof alignment to return it to its original shape now that the late-nineteenth-century guttering has been removed.

13 MARCH

In a farming community, everyone hopes for rain. Everyone except us. Today, the farmers' prayers have been answered. Bad news for Purnon. With the guttering removed on the east side of the château and the tarpaulins battered by high winds, it's a full-time job to keep the château protected. The plastic sheeting on the floor of the *grenier* and the second level offer adequate protection against light rain, but in a heavy downpour, this system is quickly overwhelmed. We empty and reposition buckets and try our best to keep the plastic in place. It's a forlorn task - small progress in one place is undermined by a terrible new leak somewhere else. We do the best we can.

14 MARCH

I'm up a ladder trimming our lime trees when Mayor Francis Siclet and one of his deputies drop by for a visit. They've come to admire the scaffolding and see the work so far. Over coffee, Francis regales us with stories of local people replete with impersonations that have us in stitches. I'm sure he has a wonderful rendition of my appalling French accent down pat. I'll ask to hear it one day.

15 MARCH

We're off to the Soporen workshop to view the quarried *tuffeau* stone being worked into the shapes and patterns that will adorn the façades. It's extraordinary. Some of the corner blocks weigh over 850 kilograms. While huge chainsaws make the larger cuts, the more detailed work is done by the stonemasons using hand tools that have changed little in hundreds of years. The care taken in perfecting details that will sit fourteen metres above ground level and, in some cases, be invisible to the naked eye is astounding.

Carved stone pieces arrive from the Soporen workshop.

18 MARCH

Happy birthday, Truffe!

Eve has arrived for the weekend armed with a bottle of champagne. She is Truffe's best friend.

José, Eve, Flick and I raise a glass to Mademoiselle Truffe. She appears somewhat nonplussed.

Truffe approaches everything in life with an unconcealed enthusiasm that makes my heart sing. She has absolutely no poker face. None. When she is happy and excited, she jumps literally for joy. She bounces blissfully through our daffodil fields in a state of euphoria. Her tail wags uncontrollably.

When she is perplexed, she tilts her head in a look of such perfect confusion that I become self-conscious about whatever I'm doing that might have prompted this reaction.

Exhausted, she collapses in a state of complete indignity, her paws askew, shamelessly arranged wherever she finds herself.

We issue all her commands in French – *assis* (sit), *couché* (down), *pas bouger* (stay), *viens* (come). Maybe it's my own paranoia but I can't help but detect a withering contempt for my terrible accent.

She is a completely social animal and cannot bear to be alone. She would rather be cold, cramped and uncomfortable so long as she is with or near us. In turn, we cannot bear to abandon her, such is her joy and relief when we finally return. She becomes our near-constant companion.

France is a country of dog lovers. Your dog can accompany you to a restaurant or bar and the waiter will arrive unprompted with a *gamelle* of water for your faithful companion. She can sit next to you on a train. In Australia, I would be quite shocked if a dog sidled up beside me in a shop. In France, it is perfectly normal.

Although she is only one year old, I find myself hoping that I can be as happy in the moment as Mademoiselle Truffe.

She would rather be cold, cramped and uncomfortable so long as she is with or near us.

Mademoiselle Truffe. Never shy when the camera is near.

29 MARCH

We set to work clearing the village gate. After removing weeds, we clear the surrounding walls. Tearing off the ivy is always delicate work: it has to go or it will embed itself in the stone and eventually destroy the wall, but pull too hard and the stone will come down with it. We cut overhanging branches that could wreak havoc if they fell in high winds. But our real motivation today is the installation of signage on the gate columns.

Firstly, we have to replace the faded *propriété privée* (private property) sign. We're starting to generate a fair amount of media, and people are coming from across the region and landing unannounced on our doorstep. We've tried to be accommodating, but it's becoming downright dangerous with heavy machinery on site. I'm a little sceptical that the private property sign will deter tourists.

The second sign is the official designation of our property as a *monument historique*. It's a condition of our funding agreement with the French government that we display the sign. And, in one of those cheeky arrangements that characterise governments across the globe, the sign must be supplied by the government's chosen monopoly provider at an eye-watering price.

The logo is based on the design of the labyrinth that sat on the floor of the cathedral at Reims and can be spotted at the entrance to historic buildings across France. Despite the château having been heritage-listed for over fifty years, this is the first time it has carried the official signage.

1 APRIL

Purnon's model farm sits around the *basse-cour* and houses chicken coops, pigpens, a sheep pen and a huge barn filled with hundreds of bales of hay. They are old stone buildings with, it has to be said, a certain rustic charm. But the farm is in a terrible state. Roofs have collapsed on several of the buildings. The immense barn would have originally had a clay tile roof, but in recent decades it was replaced with corrugated iron. It looks terrible given the historic buildings close by. We hope that one day we can restore it.

We've donated the bales of hay to a local equestrian centre, and tractors towing huge trailers arrive to cart them away. José and I then demolish an old wooden structure inside the *hangar* (barn). Later I cut out the metal sheep pens at the back and trailer-loads of junk are removed so that we can finally gain access to the buildings.

Then José and I cut the sizable trees growing out of several of the old stone buildings. A decade ago you could have cut them with a set of strong secateurs - today a chainsaw is needed to bring down trees that have grown to several storeys in height. I'm learning from watching José. He brings them down in sections and uses ropes and tension straps to control the direction of fall. It's a real skill to fell the trees in a confined space without damaging the buildings or yourself.

The next step is concreting the floor of the huge *hangar* so that we can park tractors and store some of our other equipment there. Alain Costa has devised a clever low wall to partly conceal the visual impact of the concreting, recycling stone from the demolished *hangar* that was endangering the *chai*. Other pieces of the stone have been sent over to the Château de la Tour-de-Ry to create pleasing edgings for an ornamental garden that Pierre and Axelle are building. The concrete pour is completed and the new wall is finished. It's great to see order returning to this section of the property.

These Pierre de Bourgogne tiles were leftover from the surfacing of Purnon's entrée and dining room. How long have they laid here in the attic of *communs ouest*?

4 APRIL

A momentous day on our journey to save Purnon. The four huge 850-kilogram corner *corniches* are to be lifted into position on the eastern side of the château by a massive sixty-metre crane.

We've assembled a crowd to witness this moment in history. The indomitable Nicole de Rochequairie and Alain Costa arrive. José is here, which seems fitting as he has shared so much of this journey with us. Izzy pops in with her new puppy and Crispin is on hand to enjoy this milestone. The team from Soporen has invited their office staff. We serve coffee and croissants.

A blue sky provides the perfect backdrop as the crane arrives. A debate erupts as Nicole and Alain protest that this enormous and ponderous beast threatens the fragile tunnels under the *terrasse*. The team amend its plan and soon the first piece is raised. Despite the perfect weather conditions, it swings disconcertingly. The crew on the scaffolding uses hand signals to direct the operator in the cabin. Any mistake could take out the scaffolding structure with tragic results or alternatively destroy the roof frame. French profanities are exchanged liberally but the enormous stone piece edges perfectly into place. There is relief all round.

The next piece is more difficult as the position of the crane means the operator has no direct line of sight. Flick is livestreaming to thousands of our followers on Instagram and it's all a stark contrast to how this monumental task would have been executed when the château was first constructed at the end of the eighteenth century.

I mount the staircase to the second floor. A window affords a great vantage point from which to film the next piece being edged into place. I'm perched on a nineteenth-century ladder that the workers have placed on the windowsill to allow access from the scaffolding directly into the château. Leaning precariously out of the window, I'm in the perfect position to capture the action as the third stone arrives at the château façade. At that precise moment, the ladder gives way and I plunge ineptly back into the room.

There is an apprehensive pause from the stonemasons on the scaffolding who hear the commotion. And then laughter as they realise what has happened. My iPhone has captured the exact moment of my humiliating fall for posterity.

Thankfully, the stone *corniche* descends more safely and elegantly than I do.

A MOMENTOUS DAY ON OUR JOURNEY TO SAVE PURNON.

Purnon's stone corniches.

7 APRIL

We awake after a brutal night of rain and high winds. With half the roof removed, the roof tarpaulins and plastic sheeting on the attic floors offer scant protection when the weather comes in. At night, there is nothing we can do. When morning arrives, we survey the damage.

The workers arrive as usual at 7 am. As their tools kick into life, it's a psychological relief for us to at least know that the works are progressing step by step every day. A little closer to our goal.

We will have to clear the park and driveway of fallen branches. José and I set to work on two massive trees. One was already braced against the other, the victim of a much earlier storm, but the latest gusts have brought them both crashing down. It takes us all afternoon to cut and clear them away with the tractor.

It's a psychological relief for us to at least know that the works are progressing step by step every day.

8 APRIL

The high winds and rain were not a one-off event but rather presaged the arrival of Tempête Diego. Any weather event that warrants its own designation immediately raises both my respect and apprehension. Heavy rain and savage winds continue. Gaps in the tarpaulins are unavoidable and water is getting in. Small amounts rest harmlessly on the plastic sheeting, but in certain places waterfalls appear and we hastily rearrange the buckets to capture and clear as much as possible. When morning arrives, I ascend the staircase with a rising dread and inspect the havoc wrought by the overnight winds. Again, the workers are already on site. Despite the screaming gusts, one is attached to the roof frame repairing and repositioning the tarpaulins. *'Ça va?'* I ask. *'Ça va,'* he replies unconvincingly. *'Et vous?'* I shake my head and shrug my shoulders as the winds howl through the *grenier*. The winds pound us all day as we empty and rearrange the buckets. Sometimes the tarpaulins help and we are spared huge water inundations. In other places, a misplaced tarpaulin channels the water to some previously spared location with devastating results. It's a Sisyphean task but we just have to keep going.

The team from Métiers du Bois works on the château's *charpente*.

The *étude diagnostic* will answer questions about where
many of the château's furnishings were originally housed.

14 APRIL

The first step in any works undertaken by our heritage architect is the preparation of an *étude diagnostic* (diagnostic study) to ascertain the true state of the building in question and its actual heritage features. Centuries of restoration and alteration mean that significant analysis is often required to understand how the building was originally designed. For example, the addition of zinc guttering at the end of the nineteenth century substantially altered the alignment of the château roof. Tiling on floors can sometimes give a hint as to whether certain rooms were designed with built-in furnishings that have since been removed. By scraping away recent paint layers we can find the original hues. Documents like floor plans or even the original architect's daily logbooks can tell us many things about the building's construction. Very old photographs or vintage postcards can also give us clues.

But a key element is the creation of three-dimensional images of the building from which the architect and the specialist trades can work.

Guy Rebière will be staying with us for the next few days. He first came in 2020 when he completed the specialist images for the *étude diagnostic*, using drones to capture the true state of the slate roof and a camera alongside a special laser scanner to record the condition of the wooden roof frame and areas where deformation in the roof pitch had occurred. His three-dimensional images were vital in enabling Monsieur Didier and his team to prepare and cost the stage one works and in allowing the companies to plan the works.

He's back now to commence work on the interior study that will form the first step of stage two. For Flick and me, it's a vital step. We've been living in a cold, uncomfortable and somewhat dangerous space for two years now. The interior works offer the prospect of some comfort for us as well as family and friends. They also offer the chance to finally work on the château's principal rooms: the *grand salon* and its *antichambre*, the *bibliothèque*, the *salle à manger*, the *salon d'hiver* and the entrance with its splendid staircase. In a way, it's what we came here to do.

This time Monsieur Rebière uses the laser scanner in each of the château's one hundred and five rooms as well as the various staircases and many cupboard voids. The larger rooms take around thirty minutes each to photograph the millions of impressions as the infrared light beam bounces off the scanner's spinning mirror. Millions of data points are captured and the resultant images are accurate to within a millimetre. Traditionally, this work would have been done using tape measures and various other tools and have taken weeks or months in a château the size of Purnon.

Monsieur Rebière's images will be the vital first step in preparing the plan to restore Purnon's interiors.

The goal is not always to seek to recreate what was original. Some aspects of modern life, such as plumbing, electricity and efficient heating systems, constitute welcome advances. But many things can be saved, rediscovered or even recreated. It is, after all, a heritage project on a listed building.

15 APRIL

The restoration of the bedroom and bathroom on the first floor is proving a major headache. When we set out to have the two rooms ready for the arrival of Flick's parents at the end of April, it seemed straightforward. We had given ourselves several months and the schedule of tasks seemed pretty clear. But as soon as we set to work on clearing the bathroom and assessing the floor, the problems started to mount. The parquetry beneath the bath was rotten from the leaky tub and had to be replaced. But as soon as the boards were lifted and the state of the huge support beams underneath could be seen for the first time, we knew we had a big problem on our hands. With three of the beams now replaced, it was obvious that it would be far better to lay new parquetry in the entire bathroom rather than just patch certain sections.

Crispin generously gifted sufficient solid oak tongue-and-groove boards to complete the room. But now a section of the wall panelling that we had believed could be patched and repaired also needs to be replaced. At least replacing the floor and portions of the wood panelling gives us a chance to install insulation and reduce draughts in that corner of the château.

Monsieur Didier arrived today to inspect the final paint colours selected for the bedroom. Two colours with a subtle contrast have been applied following a rigorous preparation of the *boiseries* – cleaning, light sanding and then the application of two primer layers. The paints look amazing, but the colour selection is wrong. For the late eighteenth century, the contrast should be very subtle. The tests were done in the middle of winter when the room was much darker and without the benefit of the undercoating, and the resultant colour contrast is too strong.

We're heartbroken. The change will cause delay, but we want to get the right result.

While we await the arrival of the reordered paints, we set to work on restoring the cast-iron bathtub. Most of the brass pipes and fittings can be reused with cleaning and minor repairs and soldering. We clean with vinegar to remove calcium build-up and then gently sand away the chrome with a high-grit sandpaper to reveal the original brass. The claw feet are removed and carefully painted, as is the outside of the tub itself. The enamel is cleaned. Then the bath and all of its fittings are reassembled and finally ready to be installed. Compared to the rusty, leaky tub we started with, our restored bath looks amazing.

We're heartbroken. The change will cause delay, but we want to get the right result.

Flick applies the final touches to the first-floor bedroom.

20 APRIL

This evening we present by video conference to the jury awarding a grant for restoring sculptures.

The prize is normally reserved for garden sculptures, but this year, based on the urging of our architect, the philanthropic fund that supports the grant has expressed a willingness to consider an application for the royal busts of Louis XV and Henri IV that originally sat upon the château roof.

The panel, comprising *patrimoine* experts, sculptors and representatives of the fund, listen attentively to Monsieur Didier's meticulous presentation. He outlines the history of the château, our enormous restoration project and the discovery of the various pieces of the busts. Alongside the research that revealed their original location, he also itemises the costings that have been received for their restoration as well as the cost and work for the initial stage of protecting the last vestiges of the two lions that guard the bridge at the back of the château. They ask Monsieur Didier several technical questions regarding the stone that will be used and the château's precise heritage classification. Then Flick provides an impassioned appeal outlining our journey so far to save Purnon. They promise to respond to our application shortly. Sadly, a few weeks later we learn that we have been unsuccessful.

22 APRIL

The *comité des fêtes* of the Verrue village has organised a progressive dinner around the commune and asked if we can host the cheese course on the *cour d'honneur* at Purnon. We're thrilled to be able to share the château with local people in this way. Tomorrow at around dusk, we're told we can expect about eighty locals to arrive on our front lawn.

Cutting the grass, I notice the telltale signs of *pyrale du bois* (box tree moth) on our hedges. Panic sets in. In larva form, these tiny green insects with black heads can consume hedges in a matter of days or even hours. In some cases, the hedges never recover.

We've been attacked before and we know what to do. First, we spend several hours trimming the hedges. This kills many and reduces the foliage that they are attacking. We then set out pheromone traps. We should have done this weeks ago. They target the adult males and are very effective. Finally, we thoroughly spray the hedges. This should kill the remaining larvae. Over the coming months we must be constantly vigilant.

Purnon's lions stand sentinel over our *parc anglais*.

23 APRIL

The team from the *comité des fêtes* arrives with a truck to set up the tent, tables and lighting for tonight's event. After an *entrée* and glass of wine, the hikers will depart from the *salle des fêtes* in the village and walk about ten kilometres. They'll stop for dinner at a local farm and then arrive at the château for the cheese course before returning to the *salle des fêtes* for dessert. This being France, wine is served liberally throughout the various courses, and as the sun sets, cheerful locals, many in high-vis gear and with walking poles, start appearing on the *cour d'honneur*. Well over a hundred people are participating, and they gawk at the immense scaffolding as the scale of the works sinks in.

It's fun listening to them chatting with one another. In the city, social chitchat often starts with enquiries about professions. Here in a tiny community like Verrue, it's a race to uncover someone's surname from which a myriad of social connections can be traced. 'Oh, you're a Moreau? Is your brother Thibault? I went to school with him in Loudun. Is he still living in Berthegon?'

It seems that everyone is connected in some way to everyone else, and many of these connections have some historical overlap with the château. It must have been such a lively place in its heyday, but these memories are fading. Many of the people are older. We must hurry to capture their recollections before those memories are lost forever.

It's after midnight when we slump exhausted into bed.

27 APRIL

Finally, after almost two years and many false starts, Flick's parents arrive to see Purnon. They are our first visitors to make the 17,000-kilometre trek all the way from Australia. It's wonderful to watch people see Purnon for the first time, particularly when they have shared our journey from afar.

Iain and Rosie alight from the car just before dusk to gaze out at the *grand allée*. Will the motivation for all our obsessive work be immediately apparent or will they think we are completely bonkers for having taken on this immense project?

For long minutes they stare up at the immense château half-encased in scaffolding and the two huge outbuildings. The *grand allée* and Scévolles forest stretch to the horizon. It's a whirlwind of emotions compounded by the lengthy and exhausting journey to get here.

The building's dilapidated state is immediately apparent, but its unrivalled natural setting is stunning even after studying photos almost daily over the last two years. They are impressed by the amount of progress that has already been made, but the monumental work that still beckons is sobering.

A glass of champagne and tired bodies are ready for bed. We can explore tomorrow.

His identity lost to us, could this be the marquis who built Purnon?

29 APRIL

With the arrival of Flick's parents, we set to work with renewed enthusiasm. Flick's father, Iain, is an electrical engineer by training. Soon lights that we had long ago given up hope of reviving are functional again.

Meanwhile, Rosie, who is a gardening enthusiast, sets to work transforming our garden beds that face the *cour d'honneur*.

6 MAY

On the façade at the front of the château overlooking the entrance, two stone busts of male figures face each other from each of the château's wings. These are not the royal busts that once sat upon the château's roof but altogether more mysterious personalities arranged in circular stone niches at the first-floor level.

On the eastern wing sits a figure with a ruff that dates him unmistakably from the seventeenth century. He has an armoured breastplate and a noble visage.

He faces a more classical and distinctly younger figure.

Their identities are lost to us. But, gracing as they do this prime real estate overlooking the château's main entrance, they must be people of some note.

The scaffolding affords us a closer view. During the first tranche we can study the seventeenth-century figure. The breastplate is intricately decorated, remarkable given that the elaborate design is invisible from ground level.

The preservation and restoration of these busts form part of the first stage works and a specialist has arrived to commence the work.

After careful study and having meticulously recorded their condition, he applies a solution of ethyl orthosilicate then wraps the first bust in a sturdy plastic that will remain for three weeks.

With the removal of the plastic, the effect is obvious. The detail in the bust becomes clearer. Other minor repairs are carried out.

He then sets to work delicately cleaning the stone lions that guard the moat bridge at the back of the château. The sight of the artisan astride one of the lions like a cowboy is somewhat unsettling, but soon we can discern claws, manes and even the tails of these magnificent animals. One of the statues cleverly conceals a smoke outlet for a chimney in a room that sits under the bridge below.

Two stone busts of male figures face each other … mysterious personalities arranged in circular stone niches.

Left: The façade niche housing the unidentified
classical personality.
Above, clockwise from top left: This seventeenth-century
bust has witnessed Purnon's comings and goings for 250 years.
The first step is a deep clean and patching.
The restoration continues, ensuring the facial details
are precise.

7 MAY

The American journalist and writer Ambrose Bierce once said that the lottery was 'a tax on people who are bad at math'. For Flick and me, there is one lottery that could transform the mathematics behind our restoration here at Purnon.

In 2018, the French government created a *loto du patrimoine*. In recognition of the need to channel huge sums into the restoration of France's architectural heritage, President Macron took the decision to devote millions of euros each year to protecting buildings in peril. The funding raised from the *loto* is allocated by the Mission Stéphane Bern.

We have spent months preparing a dossier for Purnon, drawing on our growing network of supporters to advocate for us as the various shortlists are prepared. The funding available under this program is unlike any other prize or grant outside of DRAC. We are desperate for our application to be successful. With the various cost increases, there is a real danger that after stage one there will be no funds remaining for subsequent works. We are heartbroken when Purnon is not amongst the winners announced in the first round of funding.

Later each year, a second round of grants under the Mission Stéphane Bern is awarded, this time one for each department across France. With a growing network of well-connected supporters, we receive feedback on the progression of our application. The rumour mill swirls with gossip and intrigue, but we have to stay focused on the things that we can control.

8 MAY

A little late but we've almost completed the restoration of the bedroom and bathroom that we have been working on for Flick's parents. The reordered paint colours arrived last week and the painting has finally been completed.

In hindsight, we may not have picked the ideal rooms to start on. Laser measures have revealed a disconcerting drop in the floor level, which has in turn disturbed the alignment of the wood panelling on the walls. It has made hanging the wallpaper and aligning the repeating patterns a real challenge. But with José, Iain and Rosie working with us, the finish line is finally in sight.

Today the electrician and plumber arrive. The lights and power point facings can finally be attached and the light fittings hung. The new oak floor in the bathroom has been stained, so the bath, taps, sink and toilet can all be installed. Some replacement skirting boards and *boiseries* are attached. The doors have been carefully sanded, patched and painted in our workshop and can now be reinstalled. Curtain railings and tiebacks are placed and the curtains hung. A mirror is restored into the wood panelling above the fireplace. The final step is returning the wooden edges that frame the wallpaper panels. *Et voilà* – our first bedroom and bathroom! Despite all the hurdles and challenges, the care taken to get each stage just right is reflected in an amazing result.

13 MAY

Nicole de Rochequairie's son-in-law and our good friend Serge has opened a *guinguette* on the river Vienne at Chinon. This type of bar for drinking and dancing in the summer used to be very popular in France. They often popped up along rivers and people would swim in the water when the temperature soared. The bars went out of fashion for a time but are now enjoying a bit of a revival.

As a *comtesse*, Nicole normally wouldn't be caught dead frequenting such an establishment. But it's family so we drag her along with Flick's parents and José.

The bar is bathed in late-afternoon sunlight with breathtaking views of the Chinon fortress on the cliffs above us. It's a magical setting, and over a glass of rosé Nicole outlines the history of *guinguettes* during their heyday, a popular haunt for impressionist painters along the banks of the river Marne near Paris.

The bar is bathed in late-afternoon sunlight with breathtaking views of the Chinon fortress on the cliffs above us.

Even the fortress at Chinon seems to lean in to listen to La Comtesse Nicole de Rochequairie.

16 MAY

I am in awe of the artisans working on Purnon's façades and roofs.

Our stonemasons must carefully replace hundreds of stone blocks. Many of them are intricately carved and shaped. Some arrive from the atelier with the shapes already formed, others are carefully sculpted on site or even in situ. First, the old, degraded stone must be chiselled out. Then the new stone can be carefully guided into place. Wooden wedges, some only a few millimetres thick, ensure the stone is positioned with absolute precision. The lime mortar is applied and then, several days later, carefully cleaned after it has dried. They must restore or replace not only straight *tuffeau* blocks on the château walls but also the crenellations that sit below the roofline and the *lucarnes* (dormers) on the second floor. Enormous care is taken to match Purnon's exquisite render, which has now been carefully handwashed. Monsieur Didier carefully examines the sample patches, often insisting on subtle changes to ensure the final result is a perfect match. We encounter Loïc on the scaffolding carefully tapping each section of the render, listening for the distinctive hollow sound that reveals a section needs to be replaced. He meticulously records the results on a schematic diagram for the stonemasons to follow.

Meanwhile, on the roof, the *charpente* team has spent months repairing the immense oak frame. Each piece requiring replacement or repair must be measured with precision as the giant frame fits together like a meccano set. As well as restoring the frame and its many rotted beams, they must also reshape the roof pitch where the slate tiles reach the stone wall, to re-establish the original roof shape from the era of the château's construction. It's an ambitious project that means Purnon will be seen in the twenty-first century the way she was originally constructed at the end of the eighteenth century. They maintain a cheery humour, chatting with each over the eighties hits that echo across the *cour d'honneur* like an anthem to Purnon's rebirth. I can't suppress a smile as I hear Cyndi Lauper belting out 'Girls Just Want to Have Fun'.

I am in awe of the artisans working on Purnon's façades and roofs.

The roofing team fits insulation and a waterproof membrane to the restored wooden frame and then a *volige* (wooden battens) to which the new slate tiles can be attached. The slate tiles are sorted, some small and some large. Some have a slight curve and are separated to be used on sloping roof sections. Others are thicker. Each tile must be trimmed with a hand tool called a *marteau de couvreur* that looks a bit like a mountaineer's pick. In recent times, slate roofing tiles have been secured with a small metal hook called a *crochet*. It's faster and cheaper, but the tiles can move and the roof will not last as long. Instead, DRAC insists that slate tiles on the roofs of listed buildings must be secured using the traditional method of copper nails (*clous*), two in each tile. It's meticulous and exacting work, performed at heights by men working mostly without harnesses. Slower and more expensive, it gives a breathtaking result that will last a century or more. They have removed the zinc guttering that was added at the end of the nineteenth century, so the new and very subtle copper guttering can now also be installed. The transformation of the roof is stunning. Although it is still hidden by the scaffolding, we get our first glimpse of how Purnon would have looked when she was constructed in the 1780s.

17 MAY

It's an unseasonably hot thirty-one degrees Celsius. By noon it's too hot to work outside in the château park. With Flick's parents we retire to Fredo's Le Cheval Blanc for lunch.

Many of the team working at Purnon are also there. Others stop by having just finished one of the final inspections for the works at the Château de Monts-sur-Guesnes which opens in a few days. As always, Fredo and Christiane are thrilled to see us. Christiane's son Gwenaël heads up the team of masons on site every day at Purnon.

As we devour the roast pork with brussels sprouts and chilled red wine, people stop by to chat and be introduced to Flick's parents. My mind takes me back to our first visit. The friendly neighbours whose intervention got us a table almost two years ago are still seated nearby, a permanent lunch fixture at our unpretentious local haunt. We've gone from being strange curiosities to welcome members of a tight-knit community in a land where we still sometimes struggle with the language. It's a remarkable transition, testifying to the power of our project at Purnon to break down barriers that, in other circumstances, might have lasted a generation.

When we return to the château, one of the masons is on site with his wife and their newborn baby, Céleste. The proud dad is showing his daughter off to his workmates and they bring her over to introduce us.

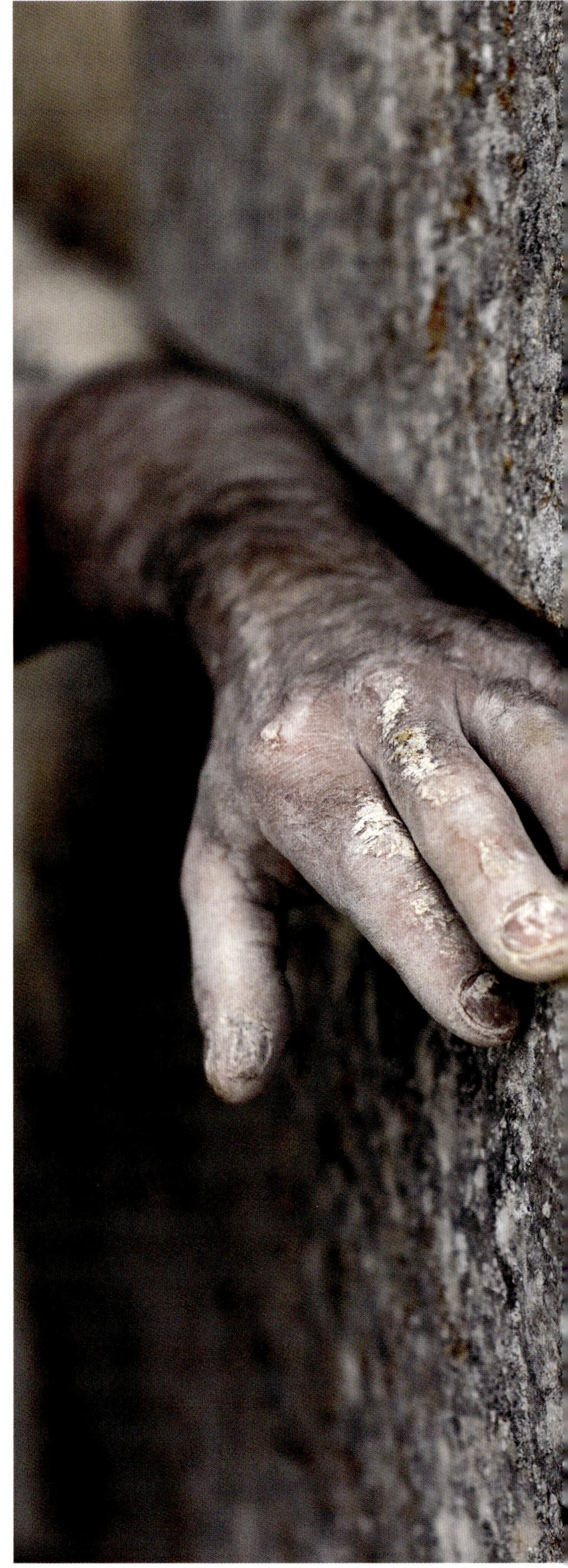

19 MAY

Two years seem to have rushed by in a flash.

From our tentative beginnings, when restoring the pool or the bread oven in the *boulangerie* seemed major achievements, now scarcely a day passes without serious progress.

Everywhere we walk we can see the impact of our work, throughout the château itself and across the estate. We feel a mix of pride in all that has been achieved so far and impatience at just how much work still lies in front of us.

29 MAY

My mum has finally made the trek from Australia to Purnon.

As she alights from the car, her eyes well with tears. Like so many, she has had to share our journey from afar. I know that at times she feared she might never get the chance to stand here in front of Purnon and savour this view. I'm sure we are sharing some of the same thoughts.

We both wish my father could have seen Purnon. My parents loved France. Their last trip together had been to Paris, marred by a stint in hospital for my dad as his health deteriorated.

Then Truffe appears and, overcome by her infectious enthusiasm, we push all thoughts of melancholy aside.

The following day we visit a *vide-grenier* at Monts-sur-Guesnes. Local people have set up tables and makeshift stalls that snake through the village. A generation's worth of junk has been emptied out of people's attics and offered for sale, hence the name (*vide-grenier* is literally 'attic-emptier'). Hunting through one pile, we come across a set of old postcards of Purnon and buy a number of them. The stallholder recognises us and explains that their family used to own the *tabac* (tobacconist) in the village. It is long since closed, but they still have a collection of local postcards in their attic that would have been offered for sale at the *tabac*.

The village is packed. Dodgem car rides compete with shooting alley games covered in oversized stuffed toys. There's even fairy floss, which delightfully translates into French as *barbe à papa* (dad's beard).

We snatch one of the last tables at Le Cheval Blanc. Fredo does not normally open on Sunday but he's made an exception for today's festivities. Mademoiselle Truffe settles in quietly under the table. A local musical troupe enters and music fills the restaurant. Locals sing along and Truffe barks at suitable intervals to 'Bella Ciao'.

It's the kind of kitsch scene that would have made me cringe in tourist haunts when travelling, yet here in Monts-sur-Guesnes, with not a tourist in sight, it's like being a voyeur into a world that no longer exists.

31 MAY

It's the last day of filming with the documentary team from *Grands Reportages* for their program about Purnon. They inspect the renovated bedroom and bathroom and film the reaction of Flick's parents. Their visit coincides with Monsieur Didier's regular inspection.

After the filming stops and the crew departs, we discuss the results of our work more directly with Monsieur Didier. He's a perfectionist and absolutely determined to honour the eighteenth-century aesthetic. He loves the paint colours and wallpapers and suggests slightly lowering the ceiling lights. But he is critical of the curtain tiebacks and provides advice about some of our furniture choices.

1 JUNE

The day starts with a visit from DRAC. Two representatives arrive to discuss the extension of heritage protections to further buildings across the estate – the *chai*, the *orangerie* and the English park. We are reluctant as we know that these heritage protections will add cost and complexity to our project. The DRAC representatives press us. More comprehensive protections will be looked upon favourably by DRAC in future funding bids for our existing protected buildings. We agree to think about it.

In the afternoon we host a visit by members of the heritage organisation VMF from a neighbouring department. It wasn't long ago that we were guests visiting other châteaux on a tour such as this.

Everywhere we walk we can see the impact of our work.

Mademoiselle Truffe providing helpful advice.

29 JUNE

Work starts on the restoration of our *basse-cour* wall. This enormous structure, forty metres long and four metres high, stretches from the back of the *communs est* to our pool area. It's a retaining wall that separates the high ground around our *orangerie* from the lower terrain where the model farm sits. Nine stone entrances along the wall allow access to vaulted stone *caves* (cellars). It has completely collapsed in one section, and several of the *caves* have ceilings and walls that have fallen and are very dangerous. If we ever want to host large events at Purnon, fixing treacherous sections of the property like this is essential.

Alain Costa's team arrives to commence the work. The wall has already been the subject of a study by Monsieur Didier's team, and the strategy is to excavate a major section of the wall, construct a concealed wall behind it for stability, repair the vaulted *caves* and install a new drainage system to prevent humidity in the future. The work will take months.

Volcanic stone arrives in huge bags weighing several tonnes each. This will be used as part of the subsurface drainage system to protect the wall in the decades ahead. Frédéric sets to task in the excavator. He works quickly but with great skill, separating the collapsed stone sections so that as much of the original *tuffeau* stone can be reused as possible. After a few hours he comes to us with a curious discovery: his excavations have revealed an old tunnel, part of Purnon's original water evacuation system. Sticking my head into the gap he has unearthed, I can see why it has remained hidden – the end that connects with the rest of our tunnel system has been bricked up long ago. It's actually a great find for us. If we can unblock it, these tunnels will prove useful for running electrical and plumbing connections to our outbuildings without having to bury everything underground.

It has completely collapsed in one section, and several of the caves *have ceilings and walls that have fallen and are very dangerous. If we ever want to host large events at Purnon, fixing treacherous sections of the property like this is essential.*

Left: The huge retaining wall for our *basse-cour* (lower courtyard), partly collapsed, with its series of cellars.
Following page: The restored wall.

1 JULY

We farewell Rosie and Iain with our first real party at Purnon. With our formal rooms cleared, we welcome guests through the *antichambre* and into the *grand salon*. Champagne and hors d'oeuvres are followed by the opening of the doors into the *bibliothèque*, and for the first time our guests can enjoy the wonderfully restored Érard grand piano being played magnificently by Flick's brother, Tobias, who has recently arrived from Australia.

Nicole de Rochequairie is transfixed as she listens to the piano that has sat in this room for well over a century; the room was off limits for decades. José joins us. He can see life returning to the château. It's a reward for our exhausting work over more than two years.

Nicole de Rochequairie is transfixed as she listens to the piano that has sat in this room for well over a century.

Flick's brother Tobias at the keys of the restored Érard piano.

5 JULY

Rummaging around on the second floor, I accidentally drop a ball bearing and watch it roll under one of our giant *armoires* (wardrobes). While I'm on my hands and knees trying to retrieve it, something right at the back catches my eye. My outstretched arm can only barely reach and I edge it forward slowly. It's canvas, stretched over a wooden frame, and I step into the light to see it more clearly. A distinguished man stares back at me from the eighteenth century. It's a portrait! I take it to the atelier and with a soft brush gently remove what must be at least a century's worth of dust. The colour changes immediately. He's wearing a distinctive gold braided coat and two royal honours are clearly discernible, one attached to his coat and one around his collar.

9 JULY

A heatwave (*canicule*) is descending over us. We escape Purnon with our friends Crispin and Fiona to one of her favourite secret swimming spots on the confluence of the rivers Vienne and Loire. With the silhouette of the château at Montsoreau bathed in the golden light of the setting sun in front of us, we strip off and ease our exhausted bodies into the warm water of the Vienne. Then an impromptu *pique-nique* on the river's sandy shores.

11 JULY

We're standing on a platform that has been added to the top of our scaffolding. For the first time we are level with one of the château's ten chimneys, literally at the summit of Purnon. The view around the surrounding countryside is stupendous. We can gaze for miles. The view of our chimney is less impressive. The stonework around the top has been badly degraded, which is hardly surprising considering its age and exposure to the elements on all sides. The chimney pots have been dismantled as part of the restoration. Some are badly burned and cracked, the victims of chimney fires from perhaps decades ago. Monsieur Didier is conducting his regular inspection with the various artisans, endeavouring to keep the project on schedule. The timeline is slipping.

Afterwards we host a lunch for Madame Françoise Vilain from the Fondation du Patrimoine. Her support for securing the Mission Stéphane Bern prize will be vital and the tour gives her a chance to see first-hand Purnon's advanced state of peril.

Madame Vilain comes from a fiercely political family and I warm to her immediately. Her father was the vice-minister for agriculture during the Fourth Republic and her brother Jean-Pierre Raffarin was prime minister under Jacques Chirac. She loves our project and we hope that we have secured her support for our funding application to the Mission Stéphane Bern.

19 JULY

The brutal heatwave continues, the mercury soaring past the high thirties and into the forties. The sun toasts our grass brown. It's hard to remember that just a few short weeks ago, all around us was verdant. Today, a haze hangs over the Scévolles forest. It's the smoke from terrible fires burning hundreds of kilometres away south of Bordeaux.

Everyone starts work a little earlier to avoid the worst of the afternoon heat.

A team arrives from DRAC to prepare a short video about Purnon for the *journées du patrimoine*.

All over the estate there are hidden mysteries to uncover.

23 JULY

One of our stonemasons, Gwenaël, has invited us to a celebration in the neighbouring village of Dercé. With some trepidation, we accept. These local parties can be a bit hit and miss, and Dercé is a tiny hamlet, much smaller than even Verrue. We can't imagine that their *comité des fêtes* is well placed to put on much of a show.

We alight from the car at the appointed hour to a surprisingly large crowd. Jumping castles are being deflated as the kids' afternoon entertainment wraps up. We spot Gwenaël and meet his cheerful wife, Sylvie, for the first time. We are immediately plied with homemade mango punch, which appears to be the beverage of choice for this hot summer evening.

Fredo and Christiane from Le Cheval Blanc are doing the catering, so we feel we know what to expect as we squeeze into a spot along the long dining tables. A surprisingly professional stage with lighting and sound equipment stands in front of us. French flags decorate the huge barn, a reminder that we're here to celebrate a slightly delayed *fête nationale*.

The sun goes down and kids play in the nearby park. As melon and jambon arrive, the show gets underway. Suddenly, voluptuous dancers surge onto the stage. A raucous cheer erupts from the crowd as a tastefully erotic burlesque striptease commences, feathers and leathers in equal measure. I am, for one brief moment in a life dedicated to prolixity, speechless. The crowd of farmers and country folk is going nuts. Popular songs are accompanied by fists pounding rhythmically on the table. The wine bottles are literally bouncing as the benches tremble. The courses and the dancers follow each other to the evident satisfaction of all. People sing boisterously. And then the unmistakable refrain of the French national anthem interrupts the commotion. Is it even possible to add an air of solemnity to a night such as this?

Flick and I are stunned and thrilled. Some of the same people who listened attentively on our *cour d'honneur* to Monsieur Didier describing the architectural history of Purnon are tonight dancing raucously as sultry performers in chic lingerie whirl on a stage surrounded by farming fields.

The French never cease to amaze us.

3 AUGUST

We often marvel at our good fortune in securing the services of the incomparable Monsieur Didier as our architect to oversee the restoration of Purnon. One of France's leading experts on eighteenth-century architecture, with his *cabinet* over three and a half hours' drive away at Versailles, his skills and experience are in high demand closer to Paris.

We are fortunate that working on a project as professionally challenging as Purnon appealed to him, but it is also true that Monsieur Didier has strong links to the Haut Poitou region. He is the owner of a meticulously restored abbey at Nouaillé-Maupertuis just south of Poitiers. It is listed as a *monument historique*. With Dominique Henriot and Bertrand de Feydeau and his wife, Adeline, we venture south to visit the abbey as his guests for dinner.

Over a friendly meal, our dossier for the Mission Stéphane Bern is discussed forensically by some of our closest supporters. The consensus is clear. It's time to back off on further lobbying and have faith in the process.

Our journey to save Purnon has been enriched by Monsieur Didier's expertise. Here he examines the original wallpaper fragments that were uncovered during a bathroom restoration.

8 AUGUST

With each gust of wind or storm, our anxiety for our *pavillon de potager* has grown. A mammoth *tilleul* (lime tree) towers over her on a menacing angle. Should it fall, it will flatten this charming building like a pancake.

Whenever we are buffeted by high winds, I venture up to the potager with rising apprehension to ascertain the fate of the pavilion. Each time it's a relief to see her still standing. Having survived revolution and war, it would be too cruel for her to be crushed due to poor arboreal management on our watch.

Felling the tree is way too complicated and dangerous for José and me. So it is with palpable relief that a team of well-equipped lumberjacks arrives with a massive extendable crane that towers twenty metres over the pavilion.

They set to work carefully chainsawing each section and then dragging it clear of the pavilion before releasing it, crashing to the ground. The men are shocked by the hollowed-out interior of the tree trunk directly over the pavilion, revealing its advanced state of sickness. It explains the disconcerting lean, like the legendary sword held only by a single horse's hair dangling over Damocles. We've acted just in time.

11 AUGUST

We play host to Pierre and Axellele de Feydeau and their four wonderful children. They've come to enjoy a swim in the early evening during the heatwave. Suddenly our pool echoes with the laughter and splashing of children. It seems to make all the endless work somehow worthwhile.

14 AUGUST

We awake after a terrible night.

For weeks France has been roasting under a savage heatwave. Last night the *canicule* broke with a torrential downpour. We had prepared the château as best we could. But with much of the roof still off and only tarpaulins in its place, until the rain starts it is impossible to know where the weak points will be.

For hours in the late evening, high winds buffet the château and we can hear the tarpaulins straining under the impact. At around 2 am the deluge strikes with tremendous force. Immediately the electricity fails and we must work under torchlight. In some places the tarpaulins hold, but around the staircase the rainwater arrives like a waterfall. Working desperately outside on the scaffolding, I try to correct the position of the giant sheets to direct the water clear of the building. Flick works inside on the staircase. Even though we're only a couple of metres apart and I can see her torchlight, the high winds and pounding rain make communication impossible.

Lightning illuminates the night sky. We're failing. Water is streaming down the second-floor staircase and, in just a few moments, the staggering volume has overwhelmed us. By the time the tarpaulins are adjusted, the damage is done.

But there is no time to survey the carnage. We must empty and adjust the buckets. Now full, some of the larger ones are impossibly heavy to lift. With hands juggling torches and buckets, we are being overpowered. We shed hopelessly soaked clothing and work stripped down to shorts and boots.

And then, as quickly as it started, the torrent eases. We use the respite to prepare for the next onslaught.

Finally, the storm passes and we slump exhausted and depressed into bed. We've had many triumphs along the road to rescuing Purnon, but we feel our failures acutely.

A finial on a bed on the second floor.

19 AUGUST

It's Haut Poitou's social extravaganza of the year and the hottest ticket in town. For the last decade, two of our closest friends, Christian and Kris de Juniac, have hosted Shakespeare in the Park at their château, a short drive from Purnon.

Château des Roches in Vendeuvre-du-Poitou is magical, with huge towers and medieval machicolations. A stone bridge crosses a moat and you enter the château courtyard, passing thick defensive walls. It is everything a château should be.

This year the travelling troupe is performing *Othello*.

Iago weaves his jealous intrigues as the setting sun lends Château des Roches a golden hue. It is a treat to experience theatre in this way, with a small group of accomplished actors who share all the parts, perform the music and even change the sets.

Despite the arrival of more unseasonal rain at the conclusion of the performance, we follow the dreamy candlelit path into the château courtyard to dine. As we unwind after another tumultuous week, I look around the de Juniacs' carefully restored home. Will Purnon ever reach the stage where we can gracefully host hundreds of guests and where the onset of rain does not inevitably presage disaster?

29 AUGUST

The best news: our dossier for the Mission Stéphane Bern has been successful!

Media descend on the château for the announcement - it's the full catastrophe, with TV, radio and newspapers. The exact amount of the prize is still being determined and will depend on the sale of the *loto du patrimoine* tickets over the next few months. It is expected to be around twenty-five per cent of the total cost of the second tranche of works on the château's western wing.

It is a massive national statement about the importance of our project here at Purnon. The public attention should generate huge interest in our restoration and it will be a great platform for promoting the vital further stages of works still to come.

For Flick and me, it is an enormous relief. With the first tranche of the stage one works already emptying our savings, plus the works on the retaining wall restoration and the cost of the various diagnostic studies, our financial resources are being depleted at a frightening speed. This prize, worth hundreds of thousands of euros, will give us breathing space to safeguard some of our cash for the interior works that will comprise stage two.

Flick does a live cross for a midday television program from the lawn of the *cour d'honneur*. I feel her terror. Live TV is not for the faint-hearted, and when French is not your native language it takes particular sangfroid. If only the French had a word for it.

Just like the restoration itself, preparing and promoting our dossier for the Mission Stéphane Bern has been a collaborative effort. When the media depart, we spend the afternoon calling many of our supporters and thanking them for their advocacy and advice. And we are grateful to the Mission Stéphane Bern and the Fondation du Patrimoine - there are so many worthy heritage projects across our region. We've had many ups and downs, but we never regret our bold but reckless decision to try to save Purnon.

Right: A delivery from one of Paris's most exclusive addresses.
Following page: The stables - one of so many future projects.

2 SEPTEMBER

Monsieur Didier arrives for his regular site visit. His displeasure with the delays and the damage caused by the placement of the tarpaulins boils over. He speaks sternly but professionally with the bosses of the assembled companies. There is no doubting the high quality of their craftmanship, but the schedule is slipping.

He is, however, thrilled with the progress that Alain Costa's team is making with the *basse-cour* wall. He notices a tiny discrepancy in the alignment of a couple of the stone blocks and insists on it being corrected. It's another reminder of his exacting standards. Flick and I could never have managed a project of this complexity alone.

5 SEPTEMBER

It's not exactly the Augean stables and I'm not quite Hercules, but the time has come to clean out the *écuries* (stables) at Purnon.

Flick is a keen horse rider. Incongruously, she also suffers from a horse allergy! When the search for our dream château was underway, the possibility of stables was always high on our list.

Purnon surpassed any expectations. We have immense stables that have not been used since before the Second World War. Instead, the stables have served as an ad hoc storage space: an enormous old fuel tank, huge quantities of wood, *tuffeau* stone blocks left over from repairs decades ago, even old plumbing pipes. The ceiling has collapsed in places so we need to exercise care.

7 SEPTEMBER

With this year's *journées du patrimoine* only a week and a half away, we are racing to prepare the property. This year the Verrue commune is involved again and the *comité des fêtes* with its revitalised committee is eager to assist.

Ampelidae wines and the Maison Martin *boulangerie* are back again. And we've organised a local band from the Mirebeau music academy to entertain guests at the *bar à vins*.

We're opening the stables for the first time and Alain Costa's crew have set to work repairing the stonework of its magnificent entrance so it is safe for visitors to peek inside.

Both Soporen and Alain Costa's team offer to conduct demonstrations of their traditional stonemasonry techniques over the course of the weekend. Soporen's team will focus on stone cutting and shaping in front of the château. Alain's team will demonstrate the techniques in cutting the smaller stone pieces that comprise the walls throughout the domain and typify stone wall construction in our region.

17–18 SEPTEMBER

We awake with the sun for the final preparations for this weekend's *journées du patrimoine*.

With the parking signage in place and the final barriers set up, we're finally ready to go. The weather shines upon us and the crowd grows quickly. People are eager to view the incredible progress that has been made since last year's open day.

Our loyal group of volunteers is on hand to support us. Flick's sister, Bea, and Bea's eldest daughter, Ami, have joined us from Australia. Perfect timing.

Standing in the car park as the cars start to arrive, I feel some pangs of discomfort in my stomach but put it down to the stress and exhaustion of getting everything ready over the last few weeks.

By 11 am I set off to conduct the first guided tour. A large crowd awaits and I'm feeling decidedly unwell. After forty minutes of talking and standing, waves of nausea are breaking over me. I ask if there are any questions, hoping beyond hope for silence. Instead I'm confronted by rampant curiosity. I can feel the colour draining from my face as I respond. Finally I'm released, and I dart back into the château and collapse on the bed. Minutes later, I'm vomiting and in agony. Flick arrives and orders me back to bed. There are hundreds of people descending on the property.

I lie in bed, still half-dressed, betraying an unfounded optimism that whatever it is will soon pass. Outside I hear the band playing and the chatter and laughter of people enjoying our park, brilliant blue sky streams through the window. Another world. I can't believe I am so unwell on this of all weekends. Flick handles it calmly.

With the statues removed for protection and the debris cleared, visitors can safely view the chapel from the balcony.

By nightfall, my condition is worsening. The pain is excruciating, so much so that I can neither lie in bed nor sit up. By 3 am we're en route to the Loudun hospital. It's not like the car doesn't know the way. I arrive in the emergency department clutching a bowl and slump on the floor, retching violently and painfully into it. Within moments I'm on a drip, being rehydrated and administered a painkiller. I pass out on the stretcher.

The next morning I awake in a state of complete and utter discombobulation. Where am I? What is attached to my arm?

The doctor arrives. Blood tests. Different theories are proffered as to what has happened to me. I am discharged clutching a script for medicines I'm assured will aid my recovery.

Crispin arrives to return me to Purnon. Flick has handled everything in my absence and the Sunday crowd is enormous. It's by far the largest crowd we've ever seen on the property.

I wander around in a daze, inhaling the sunlight and fresh air. Benji, Kate and Izzy are thrilled with the success of the Ampelidae wine-tasting. In the *boulangerie*, Benoît and Emmanuelle have sold all the bread that they could bake in Purnon's huge *four à pain*. Large crowds are watching the masonry demonstrations.

I drift into the *grand salon* and find a seat in the corner. The room is packed, the audience enthralled by an audio-visual presentation featuring many of our artisans and the stages of the work so far to save Purnon. The montage is stunning. We can see the restoration of the grand piano and hear it being played. The drone images of the roof's wooden frame being restored and the massive stone corners being lowered into place by the immense crane draw gasps from those watching. Maybe it's my brush with the emergency department and the pharmaceuticals still washing though my system, but I find myself overcome as the presentation continues.

Hundreds of people file through over the course of the afternoon, each with a variation on the same message: 'Thank you for saving Purnon and sharing it with us – but yes, you are crazy!'

There is still so much to do, but Flick and I have learned that we can master this challenge. I am so proud of how far we have come together on this incredible journey to save Château de Purnon. To have stared in the same direction and seen the beauty and the possibility rather than the problems and the risks.

Epilogue

LE VÉRITABLE VOYAGE DE DÉCOUVERTE NE CONSISTE PAS À CHERCHER DE NOUVEAUX PAYSAGES, MAIS À AVOIR DE NOUVEAUX YEUX.

The real voyage of discovery consists
not in seeking new landscapes, but in having new eyes.
Marcel Proust

If we are truly honest, even a life lived to the full is also replete with regrets. Some are obvious - a friendship we let lapse or an error of judgement that hindsight would have us handle differently. But for many, life's biggest regret lies in a risk not taken.

Restoring a crumbling French château is full of uncertainty and risk. Wise people will advise you not to do it. The safe option is to walk away - to take joy in the efforts of others from a safe distance. But for Flick and me, the allure of working on a project of passion that we could share together was too strong. Despite not knowing how this story would end, we felt that if we did not take the chance - if we chose safety over boldness - it would be a decision we would regret forever.

Our journey to date has been far from easy. The work has been harder than we could possibly have imagined. Things have cost more and taken longer. We have had setbacks and disappointments.

But it has been an incredible adventure. We've made wonderful and unlikely friends. We've learned so much - not only about our exceptional home but about ourselves. And in this modern world of easily disposable things, we are saving something of rare quality that, because of our intervention, will be admired for generations more to come.

We have achieved so much. The château itself - only a few years away from total ruin when we found her - will be saved, with the roof and stonework restored. Great kings will again gaze from Purnon's roof over the *grand allée* and our magnificent *parc anglais*, the park now returning to the splendour envisaged by those who planted its first trees.

Our wonderful *chai* echoes again with the enjoyment of wine. For the first time, Purnon's history is being recorded and her original features rediscovered, restored and protected. Above all, Purnon is again a home, as she was always meant to be. Her grand rooms fill with the sounds of laughter and conversation. Sheet music from before the Revolution is brought to life through the keys of a grand piano that has laid witness to our *bibliothèque* for more than a hundred and fifty years. We make pizzas in our *boulangerie* oven and take a dip in the pool, reminders that even the grandest homes must move, even subtly, with the times.

And it has been our joy to share Purnon with a growing circle of people. Thousands of locals have been able to admire her splendour during open days. And tens of thousands are sharing our adventure across the world, following the ups and downs of Purnon's dramatic reawakening on social media.

There is still so much for us to do here. We have scarcely touched the two enormous *communs* that house some of Purnon's greatest treasures, her chapel and stables. Our potager garden with its charming pavilion still beckons. While the plan for the interior is now well advanced, the work itself is still in its earliest stages.

Can we save the Moulin Bigeard and make the Éolienne Bollée pump water again? Will we realise our dream of restoring one of France's oldest billiard tables and returning her home to the château's largest room? Can we return life to our ruined *orangerie*?

Qui vivra verra, as the French are fond of saying. By living we will see. There is no telling what tomorrow will bring.

Purnon

A BRIEF HISTORY

Sieges, noble feuds, royal poisonings - centuries before the construction of the majestic château that graces the domain today, Purnon was connected with intrigue and mystery.

The lands of the central west region of France known as Haut Poitou have often played an outsized role in French history.

In AD 732, somewhere between the modern towns of Poitiers and Tours, a Muslim Umayyad army was defeated by the Franks under the command of Charles Martel. This monumental battle would mark the northernmost reach by Moorish forces who had occupied the Iberian Peninsula. In turn, Martel's son would found the Carolingian dynasty and his grandson Charlemagne would become first emperor of the Holy Roman Empire.

During the Middle Ages, the County of Poitou formed part of the dowry of Eleanor of Aquitaine. This extraordinary woman was the Duchesse of Aquitaine for almost seventy years and a towering figure in medieval history. Wife of Louis VII of France and later Henry II of England, Eleanor would give birth to ten children, including both Richard the Lionheart and King John of England. She commanded armies and was a central figure in the Second Crusade.

Eleanor died in 1204 and was buried at Fontevraud Abbey, a short drive north of the château in the Loire Valley.

During the Hundred Years' War, the kingdoms of England and France fought for control of the lands of the County of Poitou. A significant English victory at the Battle of Poitiers in 1356 resulted in the capture of the French King John II.

It was during this early phase of the war that the lands of Purnon (then written Puirenon) first came to prominence. The English were fighting under the leadership of Edward, the Black Prince. One of his commanders, the Earl of Pembroke, was besieged by French forces in a fortified manor at Puirenon in October of 1369, a building described as having a stone wall but no moat. The outnumbered English were gradually being overwhelmed by the superior French force. A rider sent for help in the night lost his way - not a great way to be remembered by history. Between six and nine in the morning, the French, armed with pickaxes and mattocks, attacked the English defenders ferociously using scaling ladders. The Earl of Pembroke dispatched a trusted squire to ride to Poitiers, where another English force under the command of Sir John Chandos was garrisoned. But Sir John took his time, angered by an earlier feud with Pembroke. Eventually, he set off with a force of lancers. Hearing of the English approach, the French finally withdrew, and the Earl of Pembroke rode out to meet the relief column. The siege is recounted in Jean Froissart's *Chronicles* and Jean de Wavrin's *History of Great Britain*. We often ponder where exactly on our estate, or perhaps in the village, this fortified building was located.

At some stage in the fifteenth century, a small château was constructed, perhaps within a kilometre of our château today. We have only a hint of what it must have been like from some nineteenth-century records. It had high walls, courtyards and a moat. A chapel dedicated to Saint Blaise, farmhouses and gardens lay on the same site. This was the first Château de Purnon.

In April 1584 the lands were acquired by Bonaventure Gillier, who became Seigneur de Purnon, and passed in turn to his eldest son, René, on 7 June 1599.

Claude Bonneau (1635-1720) acquired the lands on 10 May 1667 and became the new lord of Purnon. He was known as Monsieur de Purnon and owned the estates of Purnon as well as nearby Brizay and Marçay.

Prior to becoming a wealthy landowner, Bonneau had enjoyed, it's fair to say, a colourful life.

He was cavalry camp master and first butler to Philippe, Duc d'Orléans, the brother of France's greatest king, Louis XIV. In time he became chamberlain and then first butler to Philippe's wife, the Duchesse d'Orléans, Princess Henrietta of England (the youngest child of the English King Charles I).

Henrietta would become a controversial figure. Suspected of having an affair with Louis XIV, her brother-in-law, she played a key role in having the Chevalier de Lorraine, her husband's homosexual lover, banished from court. She also negotiated the Secret Treaty of Dover between Louis XIV and her brother Charles II. On 30 June 1670, she collapsed at the Château de Saint-Cloud and died shortly after, claiming to have been poisoned. The prime suspect was none other than Claude Bonneau, Monsieur de Purnon, who had provided her with a glass of chicory water just prior to her collapse. As the queen's butler and a close friend of the Chevalier de Lorraine, he had both motive and opportunity. According to the famed writer Duc de Saint-Simon, he subsequently confessed to Louis XIV but was spared.

Upon the death of Claude Bonneau in 1720, the estate of Purnon passed to a family named Aubigne that was connected by marriage to Jean le Breton, whose immense Château de Villandry with its incredible gardens is today one of the most visited châteaux of the Loire Valley. In 1771 they would in turn sell the lands to Antoine-Charles Achard, Marquis de la Haye. It was the marquis who would construct the château at Purnon that Flick and I now call home.

At some stage in the fifteenth century, a small château was constructed, perhaps within a kilometre of our château today.

Clockwise from top left:
Acquired with the château, a bust of Louis XVIII.
To the original owners of Purnon his ascent to the French throne marked the return of the traditional social order.
An extraordinary illuminated drawing from Jean Froissart's *Chronicles* that details the siege of Purnon.
The Marquis Daniel Jérôme Robineau de Rochequairie (1856–1919) in the uniform of a French cuirassier.

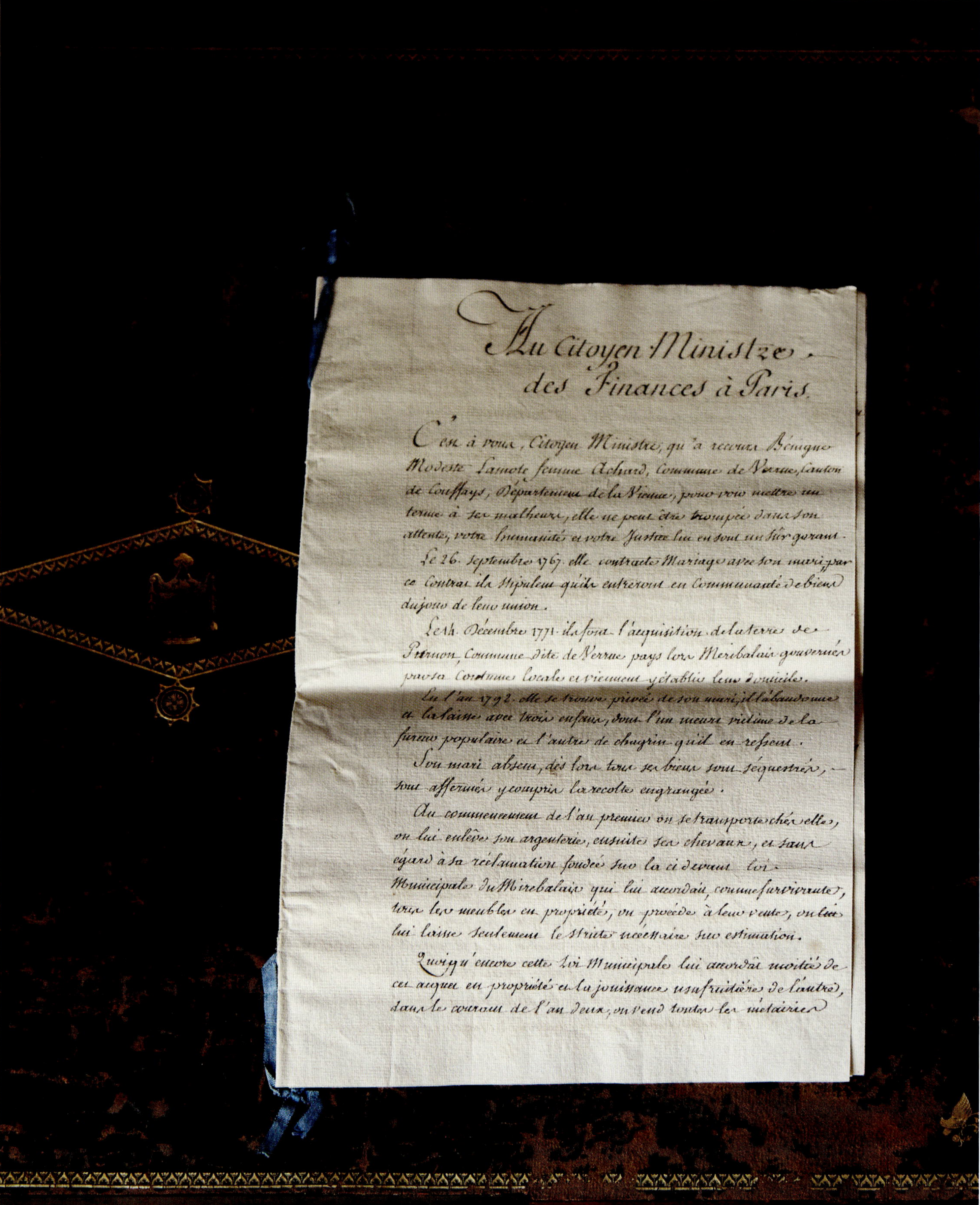
Au Citoyen Ministre
des Finances à Paris.

C'est à vous, Citoyen Ministre, qu'a recours Bénigne
Modeste Lamote femme Achard, Commune de Verrue, canton
de Couffays, Département de la Vienne, pour vous mettre un
terme à ses malheurs, elle ne peut être trompée dans son
attente, votre humanité et votre Justice lui en sont un sûr garant.

Le 26. septembre 1767. elle contracte Mariage avec son mari par
ce Contrat ils stipulent qu'ils entreront en Communauté de bien
du jour de leur union.

Le 14. Décembre 1771. ils font l'acquisition de la terre de
Pétruon, Commune dite de Verrue pays loir Méribalais gouverné
par sa Coutume locale et viennent y établir leur domicile.

En l'an 1792. elle se trouve privée de son mari, il l'abandonne
et la laisse avec trois enfans, dont l'un meurt victime de la
fureur populaire et l'autre de chagrin qu'il en ressent.

Son mari absent, dès lors tous ses biens sont séquestrés,
sont affermés y compris la récolte engrangée.

Au commencement de l'an premier on se transporte chez elle,
on lui enlève son argenterie, ensuite ses chevaux, et sans
égard à sa réclamation fondée sur la ci devant loi
Municipale du Mirebalais qui lui accordait comme survivante,
tous les meubles en propriété, on procède à leur vente, on lui
laisse seulement le strict nécessaire sur estimation.

Quoiqu'encore cette loi Municipale lui accordait moitié de
ces acquêts en propriété et la jouissance usufruitière de l'autre,
dans le courant de l'an deux, on vend toutes les métairies

After purchasing the estate on 14 December 1771, the Marquis de la Haye would build the château for his retirement with his wife, Madame Bénigne-Modeste de la Motte-Baracé. The château itself was completed between 1779 and 1788 using stone from a nearby château at Brizay and almost certainly with materials taken from the earlier château at Purnon.

It is the Marquis de la Haye and Madame de la Motte-Baracé's coats of arms that grace the stone pediments at the front and back of the château.

In 1753 Monsieur Achard had been a page to the Duc d'Orléans, and in 1769 became a lieutenant-colonel of cavalry in the king's army.

No sooner was the château completed than the chaos of the French Revolution commenced. It was not a great time to be an aristocrat. The Marquis de la Haye left Purnon to fight alongside the armies struggling to overturn the Revolution and restore the monarchy. His eldest son, Auguste, was massacred along with other royalist troops in Lyon in 1792. Rummaging around the château, we came across a desperate letter written to the minister for finance on behalf of the marquise, begging to be able to keep the château and its contents. The letter notes that of her three children, one son had been killed by 'the popular fury', while her daughter had fallen into the malaise of depression. Miraculously, her plea proved successful and, unlike many estates that were looted or destroyed during the Terror, Purnon survived.

The Marquis de la Haye returned from the fighting in 1797. It was after his return, in 1812, that the magnificent gate that stands to the north of our *cour d'honneur* was added.

When the marquis died at Purnon in January 1816, the château passed to their surviving son, Édouard. Édouard would fund the construction of a new church in the village to replace one destroyed during the Revolution, and *l'église* Saint-Hilaire still stands today. Édouard served as the mayor of Verrue, our local village, for many years. Upon Édouard's death at the château in 1844, Purnon passed to his oldest surviving child, Catherine Antoinette (1810-85). In 1831 she had married Charles Adrien Paul Victoric, Baron de Goyon (1805-51). He also served as village mayor, received the Légion d'honneur and died in 1851 aged only forty-six.

On 12 November 1850, the chapel at Purnon was the scene of the marriage of their only child, Pauline de Goyon, to the Comte Auguste Henri Fernand de Montesquiou-Fézensac (1821-96). Together they became the new owners of Château de Purnon.

After the creation of the Third Republic the Comte de Montesquiou-Fézensac would become the first prefect of the department of Meurthe-et-Moselle in 1871. He came from one of France's great families. His grandfather Henri had fought alongside Napoleon Bonaparte, was part of the disastrous retreat from Moscow in 1812 and was gravely wounded at the Battle of Waterloo. Henri's father, Anne-Pierre de Montesquiou-Fézensac (1739-98), was a famed figure of the French Revolution. His name is inscribed on the Arc de Triomphe and he was one of the elite men of letters admitted to the Académie Française. Anne-Pierre's grandfather's cousin Charles de Batz de Castelmore d'Artagnan (1613-73) is the real-life person upon whom Alexandre Dumas based the central character in *The Three Musketeers*. What an extraordinary family! However tenuous, we're happy to claim the connection to Purnon.

However, during this era, Purnon fell into disrepair.

Fortunately, the château was purchased by Daniel Jérôme Robineau de Rochequairie (1856-1919) on 29 December 1893. At this time he carried the title of *comte* (count) but would later become the marquis upon the death of his eldest brother in 1910.

His first wife, Élisabeth Marie Gertrude Fournier de Boisayrault d'Oyron (1865-1901), passed away on 3 February 1901, aged only thirty-five. Together they had four children. He then married her sister, Yvonne, at Purnon on 16 September 1902.

The d'Oyron family were the owners of a huge château that is a short drive from Purnon. It is now the property of the French state and is open to the public.

The de Rochequairie purchase of Purnon ushered in an era of great investment in modernising the château.

Imposing zinc guttering was installed around the château roof, altering its pitch and appearance. A massive heating system was constructed in the basement, new plumbing updated the waste system, and an 'electronic' method for summoning the domestic staff was added (with a box on the second-floor corridor that indicated to the staff whether it was the *comte* or the *comtesse* who was calling them). The *comte* also had the Éolienne Bollée (a wind turbine) installed in 1900.

Daniel died at Purnon on 26 April 1919, aged sixty-two. Family legend has it that he suffered a heart attack on Purnon's *grand escalier*. It seems a tragic yet somehow fitting end for the man who saved Château de Purnon.

Yvonne lived until 1957, dying aged eighty at a nearby château in Aulnay.

The marquise's desperate letter that saved Purnon during the chaos of the Revolution.

Château de Purnon now passed to Daniel and Élisabeth's third child and eldest son, Pierre Charles Robineau de Rochequairie (1892-1969). Pierre had served with a French cavalry regiment during the First World War. He would live to witness the Great Depression and the German invasion during the Second World War, including a few days when German soldiers actually occupied the château. Pierre died at Purnon on 18 January 1969.

The château passed to Pierre's eldest son, Gilles, who became the new marquis, and his brother, Jean-Pierre. Purnon would receive its first heritage protection in 1971. In the 1990s a tastefully executed swimming pool east of the *basse-cour* was added. The heritage protections were further extended but the château and surrounding buildings were falling into disrepair. The marquis' passing in 2013 would be the catalyst for the process that would lead eventually to our purchase in 2020.

By now, more than a century had passed since the investment of Daniel de Rochequairie and Purnon again faced ruin and collapse. We commenced the largest restoration program in the château's history. The French government extended heritage protections to cover the entire estate, including the *parc anglais*, the *orangerie* and the old *chai* - finally everything inside the domain's walls is legally protected.

Above all, Château de Purnon is lived in again as a family home. We are witnessing not only a physical restoration of an extraordinary building, but a reawakening of a spirit at risk of being lost forever.

The finishing touch on Purnon's sublime grandeur
was the 1812 gate completed after the Revolution.

GLOSSARY

appliques — wall lights
ardoise — slate
avant-goût — preview
bar à vin — wine bar
barbe à papa — fairy floss
basse-cour — farmyard (at Purnon, our lower courtyard)
bibliothèque — library
blazons — coats of arms
bois — woods
boiseries — wood panelling
boulangerie — bakery
boulin — niche in a *pigeonnier* where pigeons live and mate
brame — the rutting cry of a stag
brocante — antique market
buanderie — laundry
calorifère — a heating system that circulates hot air via a system of ducts
canapé — sofa
carrière — quarry
cave — cellar
cave à vin — wine cellar
cerf — stag
chai — barrel room
charpente — roof framework
château d'eau — water tower
chevilles — crafted wooden pegs
chevreuil — roe deer
ciel de lit — bed canopy
communs — large outbuildings
comte — count
comtesse — countess
cour d'honneur — the formal approach to a grand building (at Purnon flanked on each side by our immense *communs*)
déchetterie — rubbish tip
dépendance — outbuilding
domestique — servant
douve (sèche) — moat (dry)
DRAC — Direction Régionale des Affaires Culturelles (the French government department that manages heritage buildings and their restoration)
écurie — stable
entresol — mezzanine level (at Purnon this refers to the small rooms literally between the floors, which were once inhabited by domestic staff)
éolienne — wind turbine, windmill
étude diagnostic — diagnostic study conducted by an architect
forêt — forest
fosse septique — septic tank

four à pain — wood-fired bread oven
garde de la chasse — chief of the hunt
gendarmerie — military police force
gisant — recumbent statue of deceased person
glacière — an enclosure (typically of stone) for storing meat and fish packed in ice and straw for the summer months
grand escalier — main staircase
grand salon — main reception room
grenier — attic
guêpe — wasp
guinguette — a type of summer bar for drinking and dancing, popular in the nineteenth and early twentieth centuries
hangar — barn
lièvre — hare
lucarne — dormer window
maire — mayor
monte-plats — dumbwaiter
montgolfière — hot air balloon
moulin — mill
orangerie — a glasshouse, originally for citrus trees
pétrin — a kneading table typically found in a *boulangerie*
pigeonnier — dovecote
potager — a vegetable and herb garden, typically enclosed by walls
rallye — a hunting club or association
salle à manger — dining room
salle des fêtes — village hall
salon d'hiver — winter living room
sanglier — wild boar
sellerie — tack room
serre — glasshouse
sous-sol — basement, cellar
tabac — tobacconist
tapis — carpet
toile de jute — hessian backing that supports wallpaper
tomette — terracotta tile often square or hexagonal
tuffeau — soft limestone used for building construction throughout much of the Loire Valley
vendange — grape harvest
vide-grenier — garage sale
volet — window shutter
volige — wooden battens that sit beneath the slate tile roof

ACKNOWLEDGEMENTS

Restoring Château de Purnon is in every sense a collaborative undertaking.

There would be no story to tell without the support of the Ministère de la Culture – Direction régionale des affaires culturelles de Nouvelle-Aquitaine on behalf of the French government. We are also grateful for the support of the Fondation du Patrimoine, the Mission Stéphane Bern, l'association VMF and the French Heritage Society.

We thank our extraordinary architect Monsieur Frédéric Didier and his team from 2BDM.

Every day we admire the incredible skills of the artisans whose work is saving Purnon and restoring her splendour.

We are appreciative of our partners who have generously supported our crazy adventure – Farrow & Ball, Hard Yakka, Skydio, Yves Delorme, Flow Hive, Ian Barker Gardens, She Wear, Hudson Reed and Maison Martin.

And we are indebted to our volunteers who have supported us in so many ways – friends old and new.

We owe a special debt to José de Penaranda, who must constantly wonder how on earth his offer to clear a few trees from our *orangerie* turned into work that continues years later.

Flick and I would like to thank our parents. We blame them for bestowing upon us the optimistic gene that is the special ingredient for an enterprise such as restoring a crumbling château. They have supported the reckless enthusiasm of our adventure both spiritually and materially. To Iain, Rosie and Carol we love and thank you.

Just as restoring Château de Purnon is a collaboration, so too is writing a book that details our adventure.

I would like to thank Roxy Ryan from Hardie Grant and Gaby Naher from Left Bank Literary, both of whom believed that our story was worth telling. We are especially grateful to Michael Harry, Elena Callcott, Simone Ford and Claire Orrell whose design and editing skills have produced a book of elegance and grace befitting Château de Purnon. Thank you to Laura Edwards and her assistant Jo Cowan, whose photos chronicle our journey far more succinctly than I ever could.

And above all to Flick. Although the words are mine, our adventure saving Château de Purnon is shared. Your creativity, energy and love is the best of both of us.

ABOUT THE AUTHOR

Tim Holding lives with Felicity Selkirk and Mademoiselle Truffe at the enchanting Château de Purnon in France.

After more than two decades as a politician in Australia, Tim sought a new life a world away. With no building qualifications or restoration experience and learning French along the way, Tim and Felicity purchased the crumbling Château de Purnon in 2020.

Château Reawakening is his account of the amazing adventure that followed.

Published in 2023 by Hardie Grant Books,
an imprint of Hardie Grant Publishing

Hardie Grant Books (Melbourne)
Wurundjeri Country
Level 11, 36 Wellington Street
Collingwood, Victoria 3066

Hardie Grant Books (London)
5th & 6th Floors
52–54 Southwark Street
London SE1 1UN

hardiegrant.com/books

Hardie Grant acknowledges the Traditional Owners of the Country
on which we work, the Wurundjeri People of the Kulin Nation and
the Gadigal People of the Eora Nation, and recognises their continuing
connection to the land, waters and culture. We pay our respects to
their Elders past and present.

Image depicting the siege of Purnon from Jean Froissart's *Chronicles*
on p. 285 has been reproduced with permission from Bibliothèque
municipale de Besançon, Ms 864–865, fol. 312.

A catalogue record for this
book is available from the
National Library of Australia

Château Reawakening
ISBN 978 1 74379 886 7

10 9 8 7 6 5 4 3 2

Publisher: Michael Harry
Managing Editor: Loran McDougall
Project Editor: Elena Callcott
Editor: Simone Ford
Design Manager: Kristin Thomas
Design Coordinator: Celia Mance
Designer: Claire Orrell
Photographer: Laura Edwards
Production Manager: Todd Rechner
Production Coordinator: Jessica Harvie

Colour reproduction by Splitting Image Colour Studio
Printed in China by Leo Paper Products LTD.